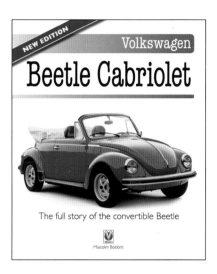

NEW EDITION

Volkswagen
Beetle Cabriolet

The full story of the convertible Beetle

Malcolm Bobbitt

Other great Veloce books!

www.veloce.co.uk

For post publication news, updates and amendments relating to this book please visit:
www.veloce.co.uk/books/V4074

First published in 2002 by Veloce Publishing Limited, Veloce House, Parkway Farm Business Park, Middle Farm Way, Poundbury, Dorchester DT1 3AR, England. Fax 01305 268864 / e-mail info@veloce.co.uk / web www.veloce.co.uk or www.velocebooks.com.
Reprinted March 2014. 978-1-845840-74-7. UPC: 6-36847-04074-1 © 2002 and 2014 Malcolm Bobbitt and Veloce Publishing. All rights reserved. With the exception of quoting brief passages for the purpose of review, no part of this publication may be recorded, reproduced or transmitted by any means, including photocopying, without the written permission of Veloce Publishing Ltd. Throughout this book logos, model names and designations, etc, have been used for the purposes of identification, illustration and decoration. Such names are the property of the trademark holder as this is not an official publication. Readers with ideas for automotive books, or books on other transport or related hobby subjects, are invited to write to the editorial director of Veloce Publishing at the above address. British Library Cataloguing in Publication Data – A catalogue record for this book is available from the British Library. Typesetting, design and page make-up all by Veloce Publishing Ltd on Apple Mac. Printed in India by Replika Press.

Volkswagen

Beetle Cabriolet

Malcolm Bobbitt

The full story of the convertible Beetle

VELOCE PUBLISHING

THE PUBLISHER OF FINE AUTOMOTIVE BOOKS

INTRODUCTION

My association with the Beetle Cabriolet goes back many years, possibly longer than I care to admit. The first edition of this book, published in 2002, was itself born out of a volume that materialised in 1996 that was dedicated to all of the Karmann Volkswagens.

Much has changed since I first began to research the coachbuilt Volkswagen, and the VW empire has grown to encompass additional marques. Yet what hasn't altered, is that the familiar Beetle – in this instance the delightful Cabriolet – remains an iconic piece of automotive architecture, revered by devotes of the motor car. No matter where a Beetle plies – the United Kingdom, the Americas, Australia, the Indian sub-continent, Africa or mainland Europe, and particularly its native Germany – the sight and sound of this familiar piece of motoring history is a welcome distraction in a world of computer designed cars which often look like any other vehicle.

The culture surrounding the Beetle family hasn't altered, nor the widespread enthusiasm towards it diminished. Cabriolet owners are, today, as passionate about their cars as were their peers, and it's all the more satisfying that younger aficionados recognise the Volkswagen pedigree and aspire to furthering the marque's heritage.

Despite Volkswagen having grown to become one of the largest and most influential car makers, the product of the firm's formative years is as recognisable now as it was seven decades and more ago. Seeing an air-cooled Beetle today, whether a saloon or roadster, going about its business seems quite natural, just as it was in the Fifties, Sixties and Seventies: one could really believe that time has stood still. Air-cooled Beetles and their derivatives do not look like old cars; they are permanently young, and so appear incapable of being referred to as old-timers.

Not everyone enthusing about air-cooled Beetles has the resource or desire to actually own one of these classics. They might, nevertheless, be content driving its modern incarnation. For them, the new generation Beetle Cabriolet carries on a tradition in the modern idiom, with all the benefits that new car ownership brings.

Retro-styled cars have a place in the modern car market; not only do such vehicles move away from an element of sameness that is common throughout the automotive industry, but they create, as well as perpetuate, a particular identity.

In creating the New Beetle and its Cabriolet sibling, Volkswagen has been enormously successful. It captures the quintessence of the car that, emerging from Wolfsburg, was disregarded in postwar days as having no future. The irony, as we now appreciate, is that the very same Beetle not only gave Germany and other nations their peacetime wheels, it allowed Volkswagen to grow into the automotive leader it now is.

It's therefore stimulating for me to rediscover the Beetle Cabriolet, to assess its, and Volkswagen's, very beginnings, as well as recording the efforts of those individuals who made the Käffer, to give it its Germanic title, possible. We should remember that the Cabriolet had much to do with the Beetle's origins, and that not only did a version appear in the late 1940s as an alternative to the saloon, it had actually been envisaged before the Käffer's debut.

Cabriolet prototypes were developed and tested by Ferdinand Porsche and his son Ferry in the mid-to late 1930s, and it's from Ferry's memoirs that it's gleaned that a pre-production Cabriolet was present at the laying of the foundation stone of the Wolfsburg factory, on 26th May 1938. Adolf Hitler, it has been recorded, chose a prototype Cabriolet as his personal transport before the Second World War.

During the aftermath of war, when the future of Wolfsburg was in the hands of the British occupying forces, it was the Cabriolet which was used by army personnel whose job it was to salvage the Volkswagen motor works. Undoubtedly, this early use of prototype Cabriolets was responsible for the roadster version of the Käffer becoming a dedicated version of the Beetle in its own right. Without the resources necessary to build the Cabriolet as a factory model, it was left to specialist coachbuilders such as Karmann, Hebmüller, Drews, and Rometsch, amongst others, to offer designs based on the Beetle's platform and running gear. It was Karmann and Hebmüller that remained faithful to the compact shape of the original design, but ultimately it was Karmann – with the capacity and technology for volume production – that produced a Cabriolet derivative of the Beetle in greatest numbers. Hebmüller, too, had the means of producing a substantial output of Cabriolets, until a disastrous fire in 1949 ultimately destroyed the coachbuilder's production facilities.

Though the Cabriolet enjoyed a measure of popularity in Britain and Europe, it was America where it was especially revered. With something like 40 per cent of total production being exported across the Atlantic, many of the cars were destined for the warm climes of California. The Cabriolet is one of America's greatest motoring success stories, as the car, lacking the size and power of most homebred models, more than compensated with its distinctive looks and European appeal.

The sheer number of cars exported to the United States, combined with the climate there, particularly California, has meant a healthy survival rate for the Cabriolet, which has a wide following and is much sought-after throughout the world.

With the arrival of the New Beetle there was not initially an official convertible model, and thus it was left to specialist converters to meet an immediate demand for the car. A new generation of Beetle enthusiasts spawned and it was only a matter of time before a factory-approved Cabriolet became available. The fact that nearly a quarter of a million New Beetle Cabriolets have been produced is a reminder that the motoring legend continues.

Malcolm Bobbitt
Cumbria

Acknowledgements

A lot of people have helped in the preparation of this new edition. I am indebted to Martin McGarry, whose original help and advice, not to mention supplying some of the photographic material, has ensured the longevity of this book. Thanks to motor industry personnel Angus Fitton and Dave Eden, I have been able to access archive material, product information and publicity photographs. The librarians at the National Motor Museum helped source early photographic and publicity material. My appreciation goes to Brian McCroire, MD of Beetle Bugs, for his help regarding Cabriolet conversions of the New Beetle; Tony Stoke for allowing me to use his photographs; Maria Cairnie for her translation skills; and Andrew Minney for reading through my manuscript. My thanks go to Ken Cservenka for supplying many of the new images seen in this new edition. This book would not have been possible without the help of Rod and Judith at Veloce, who suggested the title to me in the first instance.

Finally, I thank my wife, Jean, who has had to endure VW lore and Beetle Cabriolets to the extent she spots an example almost before I do!

Malcolm Bobbitt

CONTENTS

1 THE BEETLE EMERGES

The Beetle Cabriolet had a sound start to life. Not only was its chassis tough, it also benefited from having the robust and highly-acclaimed Volkswagen air-cooled flat-four engine. This was to appear in many guises, over several decades, powering the ubiquitous Beetle and its siblings, including the immortal Type 2 Transporter. With its bespoke coachwork, the Cabriolet quickly achieved a reputation as a style icon, to be revered by Volkswagen enthusiasts worldwide.

Two names, Karmann and Hebmüller, are synonymous with the earliest production Cabriolets. Karmann is the better known simply because this respected coachbuilder produced the great majority of vehicles. Though Hebmüller is a name that will be less familiar, except to dedicated Volkswagen and Cabriolet enthusiasts, it is, nevertheless, equally respected. The long-established coachbuilder was officially recognised by Wolfsburg, and an order for 2000 Cabriolets was granted. A mere fifty-five cars were produced before a fire at the coachworks, in July 1949, destroyed much of the firm's manufacturing facilities. Although production resumed, albeit on a small scale, fewer than 700 cars were completed before Hebmüller was registered bankrupt in 1953.

Karmann, synonymous with another coachbuilt derivative of the Beetle, the Karmann Ghia, has been associated with Volkswagen since the outset of postwar Beetle production. Construction of the Karmann Cabriolet began in mid-1949 with twenty-five pre-production cars, and thereafter, limited production of the vehicle saw an output of no more than a couple of cars a day. By the end of 1949 fewer than 400 vehicles had left Karmann's Osnabrück factory; the 1000th Beetle Cabriolet was built in April 1950 and, by the end of that year, nearly 4000 cars had been sold.

In addition to it being popular in its native Germany, the Beetle Cabriolet was enthusiastically welcomed in several other markets, noticeably America, regarded as being the car's most important export market. In America, it quickly climbed to the top of the import charts to become the most popular foreign car. For all its popularity the Cabriolet was initially in short supply, which explains why, in California, the Beetle ranked 7th as the most wanted vehicle.

Volkswagen was not alone in turning its attention westward across the Atlantic to North America. Renault and Fiat likewise saw the United States as a lucrative market, and both marques enjoyed considerable success with their small and economical models. Renault's 4CV led the American invasion, closely followed by the Dauphine and the pretty Caravelle sports car. Fiat sent shiploads of its rear-engined 600s across the Atlantic, which were later joined by the sporting 850 variant. Britain, too, fared well exporting cars to America. Servicemen returning to the United States were keen to take souvenirs with them, and that included cars such as the MG. Jaguar, however, was popular in America and it was the early postwar saloons and the XK sports cars that were in demand.

Origins

In tracing the Beetle Cabriolet's ancestry of the, it's important to examine the genesis of Volkswagen itself. The rise of the 'People's Car' from the ashes of the Second World War is understood well enough, but the history of Volkswagen is far more complex, and owes its origins to a much earlier era. The key players in early Volkswagen history are Ferdinand Porsche, his son, Ferry, Josef Ganz and Adolf Hitler, but credit for salvaging the company and the huge Wolfsburg factory after the war is attributed to Ivan Hirst, a British army officer whose foresight was to establish the company as a world leader in motor manufacturing. There were others, Charles Radclyffe and Heinrich (Heinz) Nordoff to name but two, all of whom worked to create a motoring legend.

For a complete and dedicated history of the events that culminated in the foundation of Volkswagen, and those who made it possible, it would be necessary to venture as far back as the dying years of the 19th century, and Hans Ledwinka and Edmund Rumpler, whose innovations inspired the concept of the People's Car. It is, however, very much the 20th century that this book is concerned with and, therefore, Ferdinand

The entrance to Porsche headquarters, which were opened in June 1938.
(Courtesy Stiftung AutoMuseum Volkswagen)

Porsche and Josef Ganz. Together, with their involvement in the development of a motor car for the masses, they were instrumental in the eventual establishment of Volkswagen as a company. Such chronicling would be incomplete without mention of car builders such as NSU, Tatra and Zundapp.

For years it was presumed that the concept of the German People's Car had evolved solely from the designs of Ferdinand Porsche. However, it was not until something like a decade after the first postwar Volkswagens had emerged from Wolfsburg that the full story of Josef Ganz and his involvement in the quest for a cheap, mass-produced car was fully understood.

Certainly, the work of producing the Volkswagen Beetle, at the command of Adolf Hitler, is clearly that of Porsche. Porsche's efforts to produce smaller and more accessible cars for 'everyday folk,' rather than the type of car generally available in Germany, stemmed from his own background. His cause was, more often than not, misunderstood, and attributed to his own downfall time after time, resulting in him changing companies frequently.

Originally, Porsche's interest lay in electricity, which he encountered 'seriously' at the age of 15. A carpet manufacturer had installed electric power in his factory and, within two years, the young Porsche had understood its technology to the extent that he was able to equip his father's house with electric power throughout. Through this interest in electricity, Porsche was able to apply his talents to the automobile industry which, along with electricity, was still in relative infancy. While the petroleum-burning internal combustion engine had developed as the car's prime mover, there was, nevertheless, a determined following for the use of electricity as motive power.

Porsche's first automotive designs used an electric motor to power the rim of a wheel; an idea quickly superseded by the even more effective development of placing the motor inside the hub of the wheel. It was to Ludwig Lohner that Porsche presented this particular technique of powering an extravagant court carriage; Lohner was suitably impressed and took the young Porsche into his company to assist in developing his own brand of motor car.

The Paris exposition of 1900 witnessed Porsche's first success, as he demonstrated his electrically-powered carriage which successfully completed a round-trip to Versailles. This unique journey developed into something of an adventure, as the vehicle achieved an average speed of 9mph (14km/h), which resulted in Porsche being awarded a prestigious prize. Though Porsche's design was sound, the range of the vehicle was limited, owing to the problem of storing sufficient energy, a dilemma which automotive engineers have addressed in the second decade of the 21st century.

Porsche was able to extend his ideas still further to produce what he termed a 'mixt' car: one that used petrol to drive generators which, in turn, powered electric motors in the wheels; a solution to electric or hybrid power which automotive engineers are addressing in the second decade of the 21st century.

The future seemed assured for Porsche when Baron Nathan Rothschild and Archduke Franz Ferdinand proved the potential of his design, and gave their approval to its widespread use. Not only did Baron Nathan Rothschild buy one, but Archduke Franz Ferdinand was driven in one during the 1902 Austrian manoeuvres, with Porsche at the wheel. It was also used for fire-fighting and as an omnibus by municipal authorities.

The idea of using electrically-powered cars was eventually given up by Porsche in favour of the internal combustion engine. His reasons were, in part, due to his quest to build machines capable of greater speeds than had previously been attained and, in this respect, led to Porsche being head-hunted by Austro-Daimler. Leaving Lohner, Porsche accepted the position of technical director at Austro-Daimler and began testing his designs in organised races. His passion for design and engineering soon produced what could almost be termed one of the pioneering streamlined cars, which acquired the nickname Tupenform (Tulipshape) because of its curvaceous styling.

Due to the First World War, Porsche had time in which to consider his future role in the automotive world. The hostilities had necessitated the design of lightweight engines which could be used in aircraft, and by the end of the war, Porsche, like a number of other industrialists, was convinced that a relatively inexpensive form of transport for the masses should be designed and produced. Henry Ford, in America, had already seized this opportunity, prewar, with the Model T, which continued to be built in huge numbers. In France, André Citroën followed the American theme in 1919 by building mass-produced cars; Austin, in England, triumphed with the Seven, while Morris overtook Ford in sales, and went on to produce the Minor in 1928. In Germany, Adam Opel's 'Laubfrosch' was an almost mirror image of Citroën's 5CV, but was luxurious compared to some of the austere offerings, such as the Hanomag, that were available. Success for the first BMW, the Dixi, was ensured – after all, it was an Austin Seven in all but name.

Austro-Daimler was less keen upon the idea of a 'people's car,' and a series of events which had involved Porsche in producing a lightweight, high-powered, 106mph (170km/h) racing car, was too much for a company intent on building luxury cars for the aristocracy. Porsche and Austro-Daimler, not surprisingly, parted company.

The German Daimler company was quick to recognise Porsche's genius and invited him to take up the position of technical director. Although responsible for producing some of the most prestigious Mercedes cars, Porsche still wanted to develop his ideas for an economy car, but again was met with little enthusiasm. It could be that Daimler's reluctance was partly due to a recent merger with Benz. The new management was to be responsible for Porsche's downfall, and, with him, a number of the old Daimler company personnel. A new position with the Steyr company was also short-lived: Steyr collapsed and was taken over by the management of Austro-Daimler, a team that had no place for Porsche.

After some soul-searching, Porsche decided to establish his own company. A major decision, however, soon presented itself to Porsche and must have caused the engineer much consternation. Having already produced some design work for the Wanderer company, he received a tempting offer to move to Russia and assist in developing that country's motor industry. There is little doubt that Porsche was impressed with Russia's plans, but, in the event, he declined the proposal, choosing instead to remain in Stuttgart to promote his own bureau.

Project 12

Following-up his earlier instincts concerning an out-and-out economy car, Porsche set to work laying down his design parameters. To avoid unnecessary power losses in transmission, the engine – an air-cooled 26hp unit – would be mounted immediately aft of the rear axle. The weight over the rear wheels improved traction to a level much better than would have been experienced with a conventional layout. Air-cooling was deemed an important factor in reducing maintenance, as well as providing greater reliability. Four-wheel independent torsion bar suspension was specified, which did away with the need for coil or leaf springs. Instead of using a heavy chassis, Porsche designed his car to utilize a lightweight floorpan, formed from a single sheet of steel and ribbed to provide the required strength.

If all this seemed quite extraordinary, the body shape became the subject of some controversy. The car's bonnet drooped steeply away from the windscreen, towards the front wheels, and the roofline dropped just as sharply to the rear. Porsche referred to the prototype as Project 12, and so convinced was he of its potential that he invested his own money into the venture.

At the turn of the decade from the 1920s to the 1930s, there was an explosion in the demand for 'kleinwagen,' these being in the style of cyclecars that were akin to motorcycles, but which could not be classed as motor cars.

On the whole, these were uncompromising machines which, nevertheless, were distinctly appealing, attracting something of a loyal following. Porsche's idea was for something far more substantial, although still desirable to the mass market.

Convinced that the motor industry was ready for such a car, Porsche was disappointed when there were no takers for his design. Just at the point where he was about to abandon the project, a visitor arrived at the bureau in the form of Fritz Neumeyer, head of the Zündapp motorcycle works. Neumeyer was excited at the designs shown to him at Porsche's bureau; like Porsche, Neumeyer considered the market right for a true economy car that was in a different league to anything that had already been produced as a cyclecar. Almost in every respect, Neumeyer and Porsche shared agreement upon the car's concept, the only real difference being the type of engine.

Though familiar with the air-cooled engines used for his Zündapp motorcycles, Neumeyer was anxious to use water cooling which, in his opinion, was a far more sophisticated approach. Porsche did not agree, but was in no position to argue. An arrangement was eventually arrived at whereby three prototypes would be constructed: the engines were to be built at the Zündapp factory and the bodies at the Reutter coachworks, Stuttgart, where Porsche would be available to supervise the venture.

Neumeyer opted for a five-cylinder, water-cooled, radial engine which he considered would be substantially quieter than an air-cooled unit. Once Reutter had indicated the bodies were ready, they were dispatched to Zündapp, fitted to the chassis and the engine installed ready for Neumeyer's test drivers to start their test programme.

Perhaps not surprisingly, the engines proved problematical. Before any further evaluation could be made of the project as a whole, the engines had to be completely redesigned, which did not please Neumeyer. Disaster followed disaster and, by the time intensive testing of the prototypes could be resumed, weaknesses were beginning to show in the suspension system.

Predictably, Neumeyer and Zündapp pulled out of the joint venture. Fortunately for Porsche, however, another customer showed interest in Project 12: Fritz von Falkenhayn, head of NSU, was considering production of an economy car.

The Zündapp experience was valuable in smoothing the path of the NSU project. Streamlining was used to effect the overall shape of Porsche's styling, making the prototype design far more akin to the definitive Volkswagen Beetle. Ferdinand Porsche put his son, Ferry, in charge of engine production, which centred around an air-cooled, 4-cylinder, horizontally-opposed unit. Von Falkenhayn clearly liked Porsche's offering and appreciated the car's performance, which allowed a top speed of 72mph (115km/h). However, just as NSU was set to consider production of Porsche's Project 12, political events in Germany were causing serious change.

The Ganz affair

All the time Porsche had been busy preparing designs for what he considered to be a true 'People's Car,' so, too, had Josef Ganz been employed in developing his own ideas on a similar theme. *Motor Kritik*, a magazine dedicated to the cause of motoring, had been edited by Ganz during the '20s and '30s, and the publication had become well-known for its sometimes controversial ideas. In its pages, Josef Ganz outlined specific ideas for a cheap and mass-produced economy car, the basis of which would be a rear-mounted, flat-twin boxer engine, and all-round independent suspension.

Ganz's ideas had originated in 1923, and by 1930, he was demonstrating his own prototype car, which represented all his ideals. The machine, utilitarian to the point of deprivation, sported a Cyclops headlamp and a sharply-raked front bonnet, not too dissimilar in style to the eventual Volkswagen. Just like Porsche, Josef Ganz had been instrumental in drawing up a design of economy car for the Zündapp concern. Ganz was just as unsuccessful in this respect as Porsche had been, but his fortunes were set to change when the Ardie motorcycle company showed an interest in his 175cc minicar.

Although the machine prepared for Ardie performed well enough, Ardie ultimately decided against getting involved in the venture. Obviously disappointed at such an outcome, there was some comfort in the news that Adler was showing an interest in the project, but sought a somewhat more powerful version of the car. Ganz drew up an enhanced specification which he called the Maikafer (Maybug).

What should have been a turning point for Ganz instead ended in an horrific experience. In 1932 Standard Fahrzeugfabrick GmbH, maker of motorcycles, took the decision to build a lightweight car which embodied all of Ganz's designs. Standard named the car the Standard Superior 500 and advertised it as being the Deutschen Volkswagen – the 'German People's Car' – which immediately attracted an initial order for 700 vehicles. The advanced order for so many cars is indicative of the demand in Germany for small, utilitarian economy cars during the 1930's depression. The 494cc Standard Superior was actually built under licence by Wilhelm Gutbrod at Ludwigsburg, with production continuing until 1935. Ganz was sought by Hitler's Nazi regime to join the NSKK (National Socialist Motoring Corps), but was arrested and detained as soon as it was discovered he was of Hungarian-Jewish origin. Only by escaping to Switzerland in 1934, after being released by the Nazis, was he able to save his life. Ganz remained in Switzerland until 1948, when he moved to Paris, spending three years there before emigrating to Australia.

Officially, Volkswagen declined to recognise any of Josef Ganz's claims to some of the ideas which formed the definitive Beetle. However, Heinz Nordhoff, Volkswagen's chief executive, did not refute anything that Ganz claimed. Ganz definitely did not discredit any of Porsche's work in developing the Beetle.

Taking the issue a stage further, it must not be forgotten

The familiar Beetle shape is evident in this surviving Type 32, which Porsche designed for NSU in 1934.
(Courtesy National Motor Museum)

that a number of other designs of motor car – again, not too dissimilar to what Porsche and Ganz envisaged – were evolving in the same era. Hanomag, in 1924, was sporting a rear-engined car, and the Rumpler, which also utilised swing axles, appeared two years before, in 1922. Germany was not the only country experimenting with such projects: France demonstrated the Guérin, with its rear engine and independent suspension, complete with streamlined bodywork, as early as 1926. A year later the Claveau appeared, with its flat-four, air-cooled power unit. Italy, too, had tried similar design principles as far back as 1922, with a machine combining not only a rear-mounted engine and independent suspension, but also transverse leaf springs into the bargain. Evidence that, in the motor industry, nothing is completely new.

Enter Karmann
Karmann's experience in coachbuilding dates back to the turn of the century, although the family concern extends back even further, to 1874, to be precise.

When the Karmann company first started as a family business, it wasn't the motor car with which it was associated but the horse-drawn carriage. The horseless carriage posed little threat to its horse-powered contemporary at first, although, by the end of the 19th century, the internal combustion engine had become so well established it had superseded the idea of the steam carriage. By Christmas 1895, 21 years after Wilhelm Karmann had established his family business, the Daimler company was celebrating the manufacture of its 1000th internal combustion engine.

Karmann's entry to the world of the motor car occurred in 1901, when the company absorbed a coachbuilding and handicraft workshop in the German town of Osnabrück. By 1902, Wilhelm Karmann was carrying out work for his first really significant customer, Dürkopp – at that time, a company chiefly known for its heavy touring cars. The building of motor car bodies was evidently lucrative; enough, certainly, for Karmann to decide to concentrate on this particular type of work. As a result, he was able to expand his business and,

Karmann started building motor car bodies in 1901. Today, the Karmann factory at Osnabrück is a vast complex. (Author's collection)

a year later, in 1903, Karmann purchased the Klages carriage works, also in Osnabrück, and was able to increase his workforce to eight craftsmen.

The reputation of Karmann coachbuilding quickly grew, and orders began to arrive from all quarters of the European motor industry. Opel, Minerva, Protos, Hansa and Daimler all became customers of the Osnabrück concern. Most significant of Karmann's successes was when Aga placed an order for 1000 bodies which, at the time, represented a major undertaking. Selve, Hanomag, Pluto and Hansa-Lloyd followed suit. It was Adler, however, to whom Karmann owed much of its success; the two companies established a sound relationship which was long and profitable. The agreement with Adler was responsible for Karmann having to consider, by necessity, alternative methods of body construction.

The move away from wooden bodies to those built of steel, led Wilhelm Karmann to travel to America, where he studied methods of construction being developed there. A result of this Trans-Atlantic venture was the appearance of the Adler Autobahn. The all-steel body had been pioneered by the Budd Corporation of America, and the patents sold to numerous motor manufacturers: amongst the first to appreciate its full potential was the French entrepreneur André Citroën.

Germany's economic situation in the late 1920s is well known, and the affect upon the country's industry – especially the motor industry – was quite dramatic, as severe depression bit deep and hard. Many of the smaller car-making concerns did not survive, and some, such as Hansa-Lloyd and Aga, had fallen by the turn of the decade. The Karmann company was relatively lucky in as much as Adler was its saviour. Had the special relationship not existed between the two concerns, Karmann would surely have followed some of its contemporaries into decline. As it happened, Karmann survived and, at the time of declaration of the Second World War, a workforce of 800 was producing up to 65 vehicle bodies a day.

Allied bombing rendered much of the Karmann works at Osnabrück a mass of twisted steel and rubble. Despite the damage, Karmann found it possible to salvage some of the business, and at the end of hostilities, it was possible to resume production, albeit to a very minor extent. Instead of producing elegant car bodies for the famous and the aristocracy, as had been the case before the war, production centred around creating tools and everyday implements for a shattered society. In place of sculptured steel carriages, more mundane items such as pots, pans, kettles and cutlery, left the factory.

Strength through joy

The history of Germany's motor industry clearly depicts Adolf Hitler as champion of the People's Car, along with Ferdinand Porsche and a number of other individuals. There is every indication that Hitler enjoyed a singular love affair with the motor car, and appreciated nothing more than being driven through Germany in style and at high speed. The Führer gained notoriety for his use of the motor car in his campaigning, the first world leader to do so. It's ironic that, despite this enthusiasm, Adolf Hitler, as far as is known, never took the wheel of a car.

For all its promise, the proposed collaboration between the NSU company and Porsche never materialised. Fiat of Italy had earlier arrived at an arrangement whereby it took over car production at the newly constructed Heilbronn factory which, in turn, disallowed NSU from building any cars of its own. NSU's von Falkenhayn was forced to pull out of the project altogether.

By sheer coincidence, Porsche, who was still reeling from the disappointment of the NSU withdrawal, received an unexpected and casual visit from an old colleague at the bureau. The visitor was Jakob Werlin who had worked with Porsche in Daimler-Benz days and was, by then, a salesman working for the Mercedes company. This meeting had a profound and lasting affect upon Porsche's future and his belief in an easily accessible motor car.

Werlin was held in some considerable esteem at Mercedes,

Adolf Hitler's love of the motor car is well known, and Ferdinand Porsche is seen here explaining his ideas for the future Volkswagen. Hitler is obviously enjoying the discussion.
(Courtesy Stiftung AutoMuseum Volkswagen)

not only for selling Adolf Hitler a 60hp limousine in 1923, but also for winning the Führer's respect. Hitler trusted Werlin's acumen in motoring matters and the Mercedes salesman quickly found himself the Nazi leader's personal motor industry advisor and confidant. Knowing Hitler's ideas about a motor car for the masses, and being aware of Porsche's own aspirations, Werlin listened to Porsche with immense interest.

Adolf Hitler had already suggested to Werlin that Daimler-Benz build a small, economical car and that he should be the person to convey such an idea to company management. Needless to say, Werlin's approach was firmly rejected. As Hitler's influence in German politics became all the more acute, and the Nazi leader aspired to the Chancellorship, Daimler-Benz sought to take out a precautionary insurance policy by installing Jakob Werlin on the board of directors. Werlin, knowing that Porsche's ideas for a people's car were not too dissimilar to what Hitler had in mind, was keen to convey the news to the Chancellor. The result was a command from the Führer that he talk with Porsche and that they should meet at Berlin's Kaiserhof hotel.

Werlin's informal visit to Porsche obviously wasn't as casual as it had first appeared. When inviting Porsche to Berlin, Werlin put such pressure on him to attend that there was no chance of him declining, nor did he tell Porsche he was to meet the Führer.

From their discussions, Porsche and Hitler realised there was common ground to their ideas for a national small car. The two men got on well enough, although there was no kinship whatsoever in their political beliefs. Firstly, Hitler stated what type of car he wanted, that it had to be able to convey a family with three children, be economical in use and easy to maintain. Such a vehicle should not have any of the crude characteristics which were often a feature of austerity machines; in other words, a proper four-wheel car without it being a luxury machine. When it came to Porsche outlining his ideas for a suitable vehicle, the Chancellor was generally agreeable, but nevertheless had specific ideas on how to improve the car's 26hp 1-litre engine, with its 62mph (100km/h) top speed. Both men were in total agreement on two issues: that air-cooling and four-wheel independent suspension be mandatory.

This two-door, four-seater prototype Cabriolet was built by Reutter in 1936. Ferry Porsche is at the wheel.
(Courtesy Stiftung AutoMuseum Volkswagen)

Additionally, fuel consumption should be one litre per 100km less than Porsche had envisaged, thus affording seven instead of eight litres per 100 kilometres (40mpg). The car had to be capable of accommodating four to five people in comfort, and Hitler reiterated both his and Porsche's preference for air-cooling as a precaution to Germany's severe winters. Hitler had not overlooked the military potential for such a car and suggested the possibility of adopting four-wheel drive and a front-mounted, three-cylinder, diesel engine.

A period of discussion about how Porsche would create Hitler's car followed the meeting. Porsche requested a year, in which time he could perfect the design and keep the cost of the car within the confines the selling price demanded, which amounted to DM 1550 – approximately £75. The eventual contract, in fact, differed to the proposals established in Berlin; not only had the car to be ready in 10 months instead of a year, but the selling price was slashed by DM 650 to just DM 900 (about £45).

There was little Porsche could do but carry on with his endeavours to perfect the car's design, although he secretly doubted it would be possible to do so given the price restraint. Hitler had also demanded that three prototype cars be prepared, but it must be appreciated that Porsche suffered severe limitations in workshop facilities. For convenience, therefore, Porsche transferred the production area from his studio to the garage at his own home, and the Type 60, as the project had been designated, began to take shape.

Three of Germany's leading motor manufacturers had been called on to share the construction of Porsche's Type 60. The chassis assembly would be prepared by Daimler-Benz; Ambi-Budd would build the bodyshell and Adler would take responsibility for putting the car together. The engine design had finally been perfected by Franz Reimspiess.

The ten month incubation period allowed by Adolf Hitler ended without the car being ready. At the 1935 Berlin Motor Show Hitler, proudly spoke of his Volksauto nearing completion, and assured the German nation that an affordable motor car, costing no more than a motorcycle, was 'just around the corner.'

The V2 Cabriolet prototype was extensively tested during 1936. Ferdinand Porsche and his son, Ferry, watch events. (Courtesy Stiftung AutoMuseum Volkswagen)

At the 1936 Berlin Show Hitler again engaged in propaganda to boost his Volksauto, promising that shortly four million Germans would own and drive a car.

The first prototype cars to be made available for road testing consisted of a Saloon, code-named V1, and a Cabriolet, V2. The similarity between the prototypes and the definitive model is clearly evident; certainly, there were mechanical variations, but overall styling was very similar. The curvaceous body, with headlamps separately mounted upon the bonnet and not faired into the wings, sat upon a platform chassis with a central backbone.

Following quickly in the wheeltracks of the V1 and V2 was the V3, of which three prototypes were constructed. Germany's motor manufacturing trade association, the Reichsverband der deutschen Automobilindustrie (RDA), was given overall responsibility for the testing of the cars and for submitting a full and detailed report to the Führer. Testing began on 12th October 1936, the gruelling programme calling for vehicles to complete a minimum of 30,000 miles (48,000km). There was a

requirement for each vehicle to cover 500 miles (800km) a day, and at the end of the trials, which were overseen by Wilhelm Vorwig, each car had amassed some 31,000 miles (49,600km).

Vorwig's report revealed problems with the cars' cable-operated braking system, which had been designed as an economy measure and which showed signs of failure at 13,000 miles (20,800km). Ferry Porsche was later to admit that his father had misgivings about the mechanical brakes, which were not only cheaper to manufacture, but also avoided royalty payments to Lockheed. Other problems that became evident during testing were failure of shock absorbers at 27,000 miles (43,200km) and a propensity for gear levers to break. Most serious of all the problems was the engine, which suffered, at monotonously regular intervals, breakage of the cast iron crankshaft. Only when forged crankshafts were fitted was the problem eliminated.

The RDA's detailed report on the prototype cars arrived on Hitler's desk at the end of January 1937. Generally, the report's findings were quite encouraging although there was

A prototype V30. Note the 'trap-door'-type luggage compartment hatch. Bottom: Rear view – windows were not a strong feature! (Courtesy Stiftung AutoMuseum Volkswagen)

The shape of the V30 prototype was close to that of the definitive Beetle. (Courtesy National Motor Museum)

some criticism concerning 'minor' faults. The RDA's findings, however, were favourable enough for Hitler to decide to make funds available to produce a further 30 prototype vehicles for evaluation; at the same time, the Führer announced that he was putting his Volksauto into production, when completely ready, under a scheme of state investment.

Code-named V30, the consignment of Porsche's Type 60 was ready at the end of 1937. Instead of the RDA's own drivers testing the cars, as previously, the task was given to the German army, which supplied 200 personnel to the effort. Their brief was to exhaustively test each car by driving it 50,000 miles (80,000km); between the entire fleet of V30s, a total of 1.5M miles (2.4M km) was travelled, making the Volkswagen Beetle one of the most tried and tested cars in history. Porsche was given overall responsibility for overseeing the test programme.

The V30 was an oddity, more Beetle-like in appearance than even the definitive car. Headlamps were faired into the front wings, it had rear-hinged suicide doors, tiny rear quarterlights and, in place of a rear window, there were deeply slatted louvres which provided the air supply for engine cooling. Along the roof was a deep rib, which continued down along the front

bonnet to the skirt at bumper level. Changes to the external styling were sanctioned to include the provision of a small split rear window and a reduction in the size of the cooling louvres. Wheels were fitted with hub caps, but the most significant modification was to the doors, which were hinged at the front.

A further batch of cars, which numbered 44 in total, were built; these were coded V38 and were destined to be used for promoting sales and as a means of spreading Hitler's People's Car propaganda around the world. The pinnacle of achievement was reached on 26th May 1938, when Adolf Hitler's – and Germany's – Volksauto was announced. That day was also a milestone in the car's future as it coincided with the laying of the cornerstone of the Wolfsburg factory. Hitler declared that the car be known as the KdF Wagen – Kraft Durch Freude – 'Strength Through Joy.' With the building of the factory at Wolfsburg, so a whole new town would also emerge which, quite simply, would be known as KdF Stadt.

Wolfsburg, war and the Kübelwagen

There is little doubt that the German motor industry's procrastinating attitude to Hitler's dream of a national Volksauto was self-destructive. Adam Opel exacerbated the matter further

Prototype Volkswagens underwent extensive trials by the German army. Each car had to be driven at least 50,000 miles (80,000km). (Courtesy Stiftung AutoMuseum Volkswagen)

Ferdinand Porsche looks on as Hitler tests the Beetle Cabriolet. (Courtesy Stiftung AutoMuseum Volkswagen)

Hitler discusses the virtues of the Volkswagen – the German People's Car he ordered – while Ferdinand Porsche looks on. The occasion is the cornerstone-laying ceremony at KdF Stadt, later known as Wolfsburg. (Courtesy Stiftung AutoMuseum Volkswagen)

when he showed his own prototype small car at the 1937 Berlin Motor Show, much to Hitler's annoyance. The Führer, furious at being upstaged in such a manner, decided there and then that the state would not only build the Volkswagen, but Germany's other car makers would have to compete against it, rather than share in its rewards.

Before Volkswagen, Wolfsburg did not exist in manufacturing terms. Instead, it was the site of Schloss Wolfsburg, a castle dating from the 14th century and the home of Count Werner von der Schulenburg. The land was surrendered to the Nazi regime, which demanded 20 square miles (32 square km) on which to build the KdF factory and its adjoining township. This location was sought for no other reason than that it was conveniently near to major routes of communication.

Wolfsburg's architect was Peter Koller, a young and eager recruit to Nazism, who was plucked from otherwise almost certain obscurity in Augsburg. Though responsible for KdF Stadt, Koller's remit didn't extend to the factory itself. The design for this was undertaken by a committee of planners which saw Ford's Detroit factory as a model on which to build the Wolfsburg plant. The committee, known as GEZUVOR when formed in May 1937, appointed different architects to design the building and to plan the manufacturing installations. The cornerstone-laying ceremony of 26th May 1938 – with some 70,000 people gathered – was totally a propaganda affair, with Hitler's Nazi regime in full power. On that spring day, it was probably not only the Volkswagen that was on the Führer's mind: the German army was advancing relentlessly.

Saving special stamps eventually enabled the purchase of a Volkswagen, or would have done if the scheme had worked. (Courtesy National Motor Museum)

Porsche designed a streamlined car intended for entry in the Berlin-Rome road race. The event never took place and the cars built for it were used by Nazi officials. (Courtesy National Motor Museum)

Hitler's Volksauto soon came to be known simply as the Volkswagen (People's Car). The cost of building it was met entirely by the very people for whom the car was intended; the price of the Volkswagen amounted to DM 990 (approximately £85) but an additional delivery charge of DM 50 and a compulsory 2-year insurance cover charge of DM 200 increased the original price to DM 1240 (approximately £111). A savings scheme – whereby prospective customers could purchase the Volkswagen by paying regular amounts, which were exchanged for stamps, every month – became operative on 1st January 1939. The conditions for purchasing a Volkswagen, however, were exceedingly vague. It could take as long as five years for a saver to collect all the stamps needed and, even then, he or she would only be entitled to a certificate of ownership. The chance of actually taking delivery of the car could be remote. It is understandable, therefore, that the scheme was regarded in some quarters as a scandal and a bizarre means of obtaining money from the German people. Even so, such doubts did not stop 336,668 Germans opting to buy their Volkswagen in this way.

There are those who believe that, had war not been declared, the Wolfsburg factory would have, in time, successfully supplied Volkswagen cars to its savers. The 280 million marks collected within the savings scheme were found intact at Berlin's Bank of German Labour. Under the scheme, however, not one of the savers received their Volkswagen, each of which was to have been produced in one colour only, a dark blue-grey.

By the end of the 1930s, the idea of a sporting Volkswagen had taken root. As the Type 64 was announced, so a streamlined sports car appeared, of which only three were actually built. Out of the trio, a single car is known to have survived. Intended for the 1939 Berlin-Rome race, which was ultimately cancelled, this pretty machine had all the characteristics of a true sporting car. The seed of latter-day Porsches had been sown, although Ferdinand Porsche had been contemplating such a car since as early as 1937.

The Type 64, with its rounded, wind-cheating features, exhibited all the hallmarks of Porsche design excellence. Enclosed front and rear wheels reduced drag, whilst behind the cockpit, the oval window and styling of the engine-cooling louvres were all a foretaste of not only the definitive Beetle and the 356 Porsche, but also the Karmann Ghia, of which the Type 64 is a direct ancestor.

Outbreak of the Second World War brought with it a military version of the KdF Wagen which had been proposed as early as 1934. The Kübelwagen ('Bucket car' is the kindest interpretation) instantly became a volume-produced vehicle and,

The Kübelwagen was used extensively by the German army. (Courtesy National Motor Museum)

with some 64,000 units built at Wolfsburg, was the mainstay of Volkswagen output. A small number of Volkswagen cars were produced at Wolfsburg during the war years; these amounted to no more than 210 in total and were used exclusively by high-ranking Nazi officers. A few cars were, however, made available to what were considered very special customers, one of whom was Willy Messerschmitt.

The Volkswagen's potential military use had been appreciated some time before hostilities were declared. The prototypes were capable of accommodating three personnel and a machine gun. The first vehicles to make an appearance in 1937 were rather prosaic in detail, but a year later a more purposeful design emerged. Drawings of a military version of Porsche's Type 60 were charted by Franz Reimspiess and marked 'secret'. Designated Type 62, the Reimspiess design was considered far more appropriate than the Type 60, and was equipped with such a rugged build that it required 19 inch wheels (830mm) and a central axle to prevent it from getting bogged down in soft ground.

As the design of the Type 62 progressed, so certain refinements were introduced which allowed the Kübelwagen to be extensively used in Poland, where, it is interesting to note, the ubiquitous American Jeep did not arrive on the scene for a further two years. Eventually, the Type 62 evolved as the Type

The Schwimmwagen was designed as an amphibious vehicle. When driven over land, the propeller could be hinged upwards. (Courtesy National Motor Museum)

82. Ferdinand Porsche's son, Ferry, did a lot of the work of perfecting the vehicle's design, the body for which was supplied by the Berlin-based concern, Ambi-Budd.

The success of the Type 82 can be gauged from the fact that 50,788 Kübelwagens were built during the five years up to April 1945. Ironically, it was the war that proved the Volkswagen beyond all doubt, even if the previous trials had not already done so. The vehicle's suspension system coped with every terrain and the drivetrain applied maximum traction even in the most difficult of circumstances. The engine performed just as reliably, whether working in the excruciating coldness of the

Russian winter or unbearable scorching heat of North Africa.

Although only 210 Volkswagen Beetles were produced at Wolfsburg before the plant was turned over completely to military production, a number of Saloon-bodied Kübelwagens were built for use by military personnel. Mechanical specification differences of what was designated the Type 51 included an increased suspension height, as well as reduction gears in the rear hubs.

Another success story was the Schwimmwagen, a further development of the Beetle theme, of which a little over 14,000 examples were manufactured. The 'Swimming Car' was designed

An early Beetle. Although a few cars were produced before the war, production proper did not start until 1945, on what was essentially a makeshift assembly line. (Courtesy National Motor Museum)

from the outset as an amphibious vehicle and was built as a 4-wheel drive machine, which was essential in order that land traction be possible as soon as the craft emerged from the water. Propulsion through water was provided by means of a rear-mounted propeller, driven by an extension of the crankshaft, which could be hinged upwards, out of the water, to rest upon the vehicle's tail section when not needed. The Schwimmwagen had a potential speed through water of between 4 and 6mph (7-10km/h).

The Schwimmwagen proved rather a surprise to the American forces when an example was captured by them. Not only did it perform over land just as effectively as their own Jeep, it excelled in water also, something the Jeep was unable to do.

The postwar period and the first Cabriolets

With the cessation of hostilities, responsibility for the Volkswagen factory at KdF Stadt passed into British hands. The Nazi names

given to the factory and the town seemed greatly inappropriate, and it is to the British occupying forces that the Wolfsburg name is owed.

Even as Wolfsburg was being erected in 1938, a plan had already been devised to supplement Beetle production with a Cabrio derivative, a prototype of which was prominently displayed at the factory's cornerstone-laying ceremony.

As Major Ivan Hirst surveyed the vastness of Wolfsburg, bequeathed to him by the British occupation of Germany, the future of the German car manufacturing plant had already been decided by Britain's High Command: Wolfsburg and the Volkswagen factory, it was speculated, would be of little use and should be demolished. In any event, the Volkswagen car was considered so utilitarian and unlike any British car, that it would have no use or appeal.

Major Ivan Hirst, a Yorkshireman born 1st March 1916, and who died aged 84 on 10th March 2000, had an understanding of the German way of life. Before the war he had travelled to

The history of the Beetle Cabriolet is part of Volkswagen. Right from the Beetle's early beginnings a Cabriolet version was planned. (Courtesy Stiftung AutoMuseum Volkswagen)

The manufacture of the 1000th Volkswagen was an auspicious occasion. The car is being driven off the assembly line by Major Ivan Hirst. (Courtesy Stiftung AutoMuseum Volkswagen)

It was largely due to the efforts of Major Ivan Hirst, and others, that the Volkswagen factory resumed production. Here, Major Hirst (on the left) examines an early saloon.
(Courtesy Stiftung AutoMuseum Volkswagen)

Berlin under an Anglo-German exchange scheme, arranged through the Manchester College of Technology, and had studied the working practices of German factories. Called up for military service in September 1939, Hirst was sent to France and later assigned to the Royal Army Ordnance Corps as an Ordnance Mechanical Engineer working on tank maintenance. In October 1942 he was incorporated into the Corps of Royal Electrical and Mechanical Engineers (REME) and was given the task of overseeing tank repair and maintenance in Belgium. Following the Allies' occupation of Wolfsburg, REME was given charge of establishing a repair workshop to ensure that demands for equipment and vehicles were met. Major Hirst's experience in engineering, in addition to his knowledge of German factory and working procedures, made him the ideal candidate for the task of supervising the Volkswagen works.

Before Hirst's arrival at Wolfsburg the REME had established a large workshop within the Volkswagen factory for the repair of British military vehicles, engines and supply of components. It was necessary to use local workforce to complement REME personnel, particularly as the German people were anxious to work, as well as industriously trying to salvage whatever

was possible of the factory, its tools and production plant. Incredibly, amongst all the rubble, enough plant survived the allied bombing raids to get some limited production under way; from the materials available it was even possible to produce a small number of vehicles.

From August 1945, when Major Hirst was appointed the task of overseeing the vehicle workshops, to the end of that year, something in the order of 1800 cars were built. This remarkable achievement accounted for virtually 98 per cent of all motor car production in Germany throughout the immediate postwar period. Even Major Hirst took to driving a four-wheel-drive Kommandeurwagen, one of two examples built, the other going to the French army for evaluation.

The decision to demolish Wolfsburg was consequently revoked when the British High Command realised that the Volkswagen factory clearly did have something to offer. Amongst the cars produced at Wolfsburg, and of special interest, was a Cabriolet version of the Beetle which was used by Colonel Charles Radclyffe whilst serving with Major Hirst. Radclyffe, like Hirst, was no stranger to European industrial practices. Before the Great War he was among a number of British

Army officers sent abroad (in his case, France) to discover what effects motorised transport was having on both military and civilian life. Colonel Radclyffe's brief had been to dismantle the Wolfsburg production line and machine tools and make the Volkswagen available to Britain's car makers, none of which were interested in what was perceived as an eccentric and ugly utilitarian vehicle with no commercial potential.

The question of what, ultimately, to do with the Volkswagen factory had, however, to be resolved. In essence, the company was 'up for grabs,' with both the French and Australians showing an interest. The British had already ruled a line under the affair, but it was Henry Ford who seemed the most likely candidate to acquire the company at no cost. Surprisingly, even he declined the opportunity of incorporating the company into the Ford empire, taking the view that it had nothing to offer. Ultimately, the decision was taken to return Volkswagen to the German people. In retrospect – and in view of the huge numbers of Volkswagen vehicles that eventually entered America – Ford's decision must have been one of his greatest mistakes ...

Essentially, the postwar Cabriolet built for Colonel Radclyffe represented the beginning of a range of derivatives based upon the standard Beetle. It represented, too, the beginnings of the Hebmüller Cabriolet, rival for a short time to the Karmann Beetle Cabriolet.

Colonel Charles Radclyffe's Cabriolet had an interesting pedigree, with ancestry stemming from the period immediately prior to the Second World War. The prototype Beetle displayed at the 1938 Berlin Motor Show had, quite naturally, caused a sensation amongst the motoring journalists clamouring to try the vehicle for themselves. One of those most interested in seeing the Volkswagen was Michael McEvoy who, apart from being an apprentice at Rolls-Royce, enjoyed some success with building motorcycles, before taking on a consultancy with Mercedes-Benz, advising the company on its motor racing activities.

McEvoy's interest in motorsport prompted him to suggest that a 'Sports Beetle' be made-up in the Wolfsburg workshops, much, it is said, to Major Ivan Hirst's annoyance. Although considering such a proposal more a hindrance than anything else, he did not, however, entirely reject McEvoy's idea. Instead, he passed some sketches to Rudolph Ringel, who had once worked for Ferdinand Porsche and was now in charge of Wolfsburg's experimental department.

Little time was lost by Ringel in converting into reality the sketches passed to him by Major Hirst. The result was an immensely attractive two-seater Cabriolet made up, for the most part, from panels normally used in production of the standard Beetle. The front of the car was virtually that of any car on the Beetle assembly line; even the windscreen was standard, but cut off at roof level. The rear panel was simply a modified bonnet or front panel, differing only by having cooling louvres punched into the metalwork.

Colonel Radclyffe's Cabriolet, it appears, provided completely satisfactory service, despite it having to be re-chassied due to an unfortunate accident. The car received extensive damage when it hit a girder, which ripped out some of the drivetrain mechanism. It is known that the car continued its exemplary service, but its eventual fate is unclear; a pity, considering its place in Volkswagen history.

The idea of producing Cabriolets for use by British officers must have occurred, as more Cabriolets emerged from Wolfsburg, including some four-seater versions.

There was little doubt that a Cabriolet version of the Beetle would eventually be unveiled as part of the Volkswagen range. Prewar, not only had a Cabriolet been planned and displayed with some glory at Hitler's propaganda occasions, but specialist coachbuilders had also shown a marked interest from the very beginning. Comparing the 1938 prototype to the later examples produced by Karmann, the similarity is clearly evident. Coachbuilders keen to build upon the Volkswagen theme included Hebmüller, along with Rometsch, whose charismatic Johannes Beeskow-designed Cabriolet earned its 'Banana' nickname due to a long and curvaceous profile; offerings from the Swiss Beutler company were more in keeping with the Karmann Ghia, whilst the Dannenhauer and Stauss cars resembled the Porsche 356 somewhat. There were plenty of one-off designs, but these were generally rather bizarre.

The particular prewar Cabriolet displayed at the Wolfsburg cornerstone-laying ceremony is of special interest, especially as its survival has been assured. Presented to Adolf Hitler, the car was used by the Führer as personal transport on a semi-regular basis, and as a means of propaganda at national events.

At the end of the war, the car – fortunately – was recovered, after, it is claimed, it had completed some 375,000 miles (600,000km). Now carefully restored, the Cabriolet is on display at the Volkswagen Museum at Wolfsburg.

Karmann and Hebmüller receive Volkswagen approval

Following Heinz Nordhoff's appointment by the British occupying forces to the position of general manager of Volkswagen in 1948, the decision was quickly taken to establish a range of Cabriolet Beetles. Nordhoff, although showing total enthusiasm for the

Continued on page 33

Heinz Nordhoff with the Volkswagen Beetle, the car in which he had complete faith.
(Courtesy Stiftung AutoMuseum Volkswagen)

Hebmüller was the builder of early Cabriolets until a fire damaged the coachbuilder's premises. The firm never fully recovered from the fire and eventually went out of business. The unusual example seen in this, apparently, publicity photograph was built for the German police. Note the shape of the hood compared to that fitted to a Karmann Cabriolet, as depicted elsewhere. (Courtesy Stiftung AutoMuseum Volkswagen)

Hebmüller Cabriolets enjoy a loyal following, and because so few were built, are now rare. There are styling differences between the Hebmüller and Karmann, the former being characteristic of the original Cabriolets built at Wolfsburg when the factory was under British control. (Courtesy Ken Cservenka)

This group of Hebmüller Cabriolets is pictured in the summer of 2009 at a Volkswagen event in Germany. Hebmüllers have distinctive engine compartment covers and centre registration plate lamps. (Courtesy Ken Cservenka)

Hebmüller dashboard and facia with its unique instrument arrangement. (Courtesy Ken Cservenka)

Two rarities are seen here, in the form of a Kübelwagen and a Hebmüller. The latter was a popular choice for customers wanting a Cabriolet version of the Beetle, until a fire at the coachbuilder's premises compromised output. The firm never recovered from the fire and, ultimately, production ceased. The Kübelwagen (bucket car) was used by the German army and examples were much admired when captured by the Allied forces. (Courtesy Ken Cservenka)

venture, was, however, less than convinced that assembly of the Cabriolets should be undertaken at Wolfsburg. He took the view that all available production capacity should be concentrated on supplying standard Saloon cars for both home and export use.

Nordhoff ultimately chose two companies to produce the Beetle Cabriolet: Hebmüller and Karmann. Hebmüller, which was located at Barmen, near Wuppertal, would concentrate

on two-seater variants, whilst four-seater versions would be produced by Karmann at Osnabrück. The two nominated coachbuilders received factory approval, but this did not prevent other specialists from preparing designs of their own; in the main, however, such variants seldom exceeded more than a few examples. The problem faced by specialists without official Volkswagen approval was the extreme difficulty experienced in

Pictured at Hessisch Oldendorf, June 2009, this rare Dannenhauer & Strauss-variant Beetle Cabriolet has more Porsche styling about it than Volkswagen. The coachbuilder began operations in 1951, Gottfried Dannenhauer having previously worked for Reutter. Kurt Strauss was Dannenhauer's son-in-law. (Courtesy Ken Cservenka)

Swiss coachbuilder Beutler was another firm constructing sought-after Beetle Cabriolets. Established in 1943, Beutler prestigiously constructed Porsche prototype bodies in 1948 and, in the early 1950s, built a number of four-seater Volkswagens of the design depicted here. (Courtesy Ken Cservenka)

Amongst the rarest of coachbuilt Beetle Cabriolets is the Denzel, pictured here at Hessisch Oldendorf. Production of the Austrian Denzel, originally based on the Kübelwagen, began in 1953 and lasted until 1959, during which some 350 examples were constructed. (Courtesy Ken Cservenka)

obtaining the all-important chassis; invariably the purchase of a whole car was necessary. Unfortunately, it had to be dismantled before a start on conversion work could be made. Needless to say, this did not often happen, but it was occasionally possible, knowing the right procedure, to obtain either a chassis or bodyshell through somewhat devious means. Some of the cars were often less than practical, offering little apart from extravagant body styling.

Hebmüller was not entirely new to Volkswagen conversions, as the company had already started to produce a curious four-seater Cabriolet for the German police. In Hebmüller's subsidiary factory at Wülfrath, the coachbuilder, on receiving standard cars from Wolfsburg, removed the roof as far back as

the engine cooling louvres, the doors and the rear body panels. With very elementary stiffening of the chassis, the converted Beetles were fitted with fabric roof and doors, which provided very little in the way of safety or weather protection.

Some important lessons were learnt by Hebmüller in its experience with conversion of police vehicles. More refined strengthening was applied in the form of a re-designed windscreen, a Z-section girder added to the underside of the chassis, and an extra crossmember at the rear. The rear quarterpanels were also strengthened to bear the weight of the car's hood.

In essence, Hebmüller's Cabriolet was very similar to those examples built at Wolfsburg when the factory was under British control. The main difference between Hebmüller's offering and

35

1945, and the 10,000th Volkswagen is produced.
(Courtesy National Motor Museum)

The Karmann Cabriolet. This 1949 publicity
photograph suggests that the finish of the car is less
than perfect, as the doors appear to fit badly.
(Courtesy Stiftung AutoMuseum Volkswagen)

those cars used by Major Ivan Hirst and Colonel Charles Radclyffe, was that the Hebmüller was a two-seater. Given the designation Type 14A, Volkswagen issued an order for 2000 Hebmüller cars as soon as factory approval had been granted.

Production of Hebmüller's Cabriolets was shortlived, however. The Wülfrath factory suffered serious fire damage in July 1949, and even though a massive effort resulted in a partial return to production, it was not enough to save the company. Within four weeks bankruptcy became inevitable. Of the 2000 cars ordered it is thought that approximately 750 were actually supplied, although official Volkswagen figures put the number at 696. Whatever the true figure, it is known that production of the Hebmüller Cabriolet was transferred to Karmann at Osnabrück once the company had ceased trading. Not all of the remaining order was built, however, as Karmann was able to complete only 15 cars out of the remaining Hebmüller stock.

Approval for Karmann to build a four-seater Cabriolet resulted in the model being given the designation Type 15. Detailed discussions between Karmann

Early Karmann Cabriolets can be identified by the semaphore signal indicators built into the front quarterpanels. (Courtesy Stiftung AutoMuseum Volkswagen)

and Heinz Nordhoff had been held before allocation of a Type number, and, only then, after submission of satisfactory prototype cars, was a number issued.

Resumption of vehicle production after the war had not been a particularly easy task for Karmann, which had been forced, out of necessity, to concentrate on the manufacture of utility items rather than motor cars. The first step back into the business of coachbuilding in which the company could specialise was to offer an essential vehicle repair service. Karmann also became a supplier of toolmakers to other motor manufacturers, such as Hanomag, Büssing and Ford. In order to provide a coachbuilt car it was necessary to have a chassis or bodyshell (often a finished car) in the first place. In addition, an official permit was necessary to obtain a car, and this Karmann did not possess.

By sheer determination and continual lobbying of the Volkswagen company, the desired result was eventually achieved; a Beetle – the 10,000th car produced after the war – was presented to Karmann in November 1946. Very soon, a second car was made available. The two cars acquired by Karmann quickly resulted in a brace of prototypes being submitted to Volkswagen for approval. Although both cars appeared somewhat similar in design, there were, nonetheless, important differences. The first prototype had wind-down glass in the door windows only, and lacked a rear window in the hood. Externally, the car was less stylish than the second prototype, especially in its adoption of external hinges. By the time the second prototype car was delivered to Wolfsburg, it was evident that some smoothing of the design had taken place. Wind-down windows had been adopted for the rear of the cabin and a rear windscreen added, albeit a very small one! The rear screen of the standard Saloon car was, of course, a split oval. On the Cabriolet, due to the fabric hood, a single screen was possible. Tidying-up of the overall shape had been achieved by concealing all the hinges.

At a glance, Karmann's Beetle Cabriolet can be distinguished from the Hebmüller Cabriolet by the shape and design of the fabric hood and the line of the engine compartment. The Hebmüller was devoid of rear side windows, denoting the car's two-seat specification, and the engine compartment cover was reminiscent of the bonnet with cooling louvres along the top edge. The Karmann hood was a full-length affair, with side windows at the rear, essential because the model was a four-seater. The engine compartment cover was almost identical to that of the production Saloon and the car appeared far heavier than the Hebmüller.

A third prototype Karmann Cabriolet, essentially very similar to the second, was presented to Heinz Nordhoff in May 1949. If the two previous prototypes had merely interested Volkswagen's management, it was this, the third car, that confirmed Nordhoff's approval of the Karmann Cabriolet. It was good news for Karmann when an invitation from Wolfsburg was received to build a batch of 25 pre-production cars, soon after the third prototype car had been delivered. Until this point, due to an uncertain future and a lack of raw materials, Karmann had been unable to contemplate serious future business.

The proving period for Karmann's pre-production cars was all-important. Each car underwent a gruelling 12,500 miles (20,000km) test programme, the result of which left no doubt about the excellent design and quality of the model. Greatly impressed, Heinz Nordhoff presented the Karmann company with an initial order for 1000 cars and production of the four-seater Cabriolet commenced at Osnabrück in September 1949. An order for a further 1000 cars soon followed, and another, and another. In a little under a year after the first Beetle Cabriolet had been built at Osnabrück, orders totalling 10,000 cars were fulfilled and the Karmann had become a real success.

Purchase price of the Karmann Cabriolet was DM 5450, the same as for the Hebmüller. At that figure, the Karmann was affordable and its appeal apparent from the outset. During its life the Karmann Cabriolet appealed to stars of the big screen; Brigitte Bardot, amongst others, enjoyed its charms. The car was also popular with those prominent in society; Yves Saint Laurent and Pierre Cardin found it irresistible. One of its greatest – and unlikeliest – devotees was Gianni Agnelli, head of the Fiat empire in Italy and producer of possibly the Volkswagen Beetle's closest rivals, the Fiat 600 and the minuscule 500 Nuova.

Heinz Nordhoff seemed an improbable candidate to spearhead the Volkswagen company. Until his appointment, he had had virtually no experience of the Volkswagen as a car, and may, in fact, have had little regard for it. Essentially, though, Nordhoff was an excellent organiser; an expert in marketing who lived by his results. He trained with BMW and later joined Opel: at the time of General Motors' takeover of Adam Opel's empire, Nordhoff gained an invaluable insight into the American motor industry by enjoying a sojourn at Detroit. His experience in American methods and attitudes made him the ideal choice to lead Volkswagen from ashes to prosperity.

THE CABRIOLET EVOLVES

A Car with a Difference – but still a true Volkswagen. This was the wording on the Karmann Cabriolet brochure which summed up the car precisely.

Though Karmann was the largest producer of Beetle Cabriolets, it was by no means the only coachbuilder offering such variants. Hebmüller was also Volkswagen-approved and famous for its creation of the extremely handsome two-seat body, until a serious fire at the coachbuilder's factory temporarily halted production. Adding insult to Hebmüller's injury, a deep financial crisis was the precursor to the firm's collapse. Rometsch, Dannenhaur & Strauss, Drews, and Beutler were other recognised coachbuilders using the Volkswagen chassis.

The idea of a motor manufacturer marketing a convertible version of a successful saloon model was not unusual in the

A number of coachbuilders used the Volkswagen chassis on which to build their bodies. This is the Drews. (Author's collection)

Innenlenker mit Faltdach

When the Beetle was introduced, the catalogue offered a model with a full-length sunroof as an alternative to the saloon. (Courtesy Volkswagen)

post-Second World War motor industry. In Britain, Morris produced in excess of 378,000 Minor tourers; Austin offered the A40 Sports and the Atlantic Convertible, while Rootes supplied an attractive version of the Minx. Standard, Panhard and Ford also produced convertibles of their established models, while Fiat flooded the market with its 500C Topolino, which was designed with an opening fabric roof, as indeed was Citroën's 2CV. Successor to the Fiat 500C was the 600, which was available as a saloon or soft-top.

Whilst not officially offering the Beetle four-seat Cabriolet until 1949, prototype Karmann Beetles were in evidence at an earlier date. One such car that has survived appears to originate from 1948, and is peculiar inasmuch as it has no cooling louvres on the engine compartment lid. Cooling seems to be provided by two small air-intakes, one each side of the car, discreetly positioned above the rear wing. A further difference to the eventual production model is the shape of the windscreen, which has a flatter top surround, instead of curved.

Early Karmann Cabriolets are easy to identify: look for the semaphore signals on the front quarterpanels; by the end of the first production year these had been repositioned on the rear quarterpanels, immediately aft of the doors. A point to confuse the issue is that the Hebmüller also had semaphores mounted in the front quarterpanels. The Hebmüller Cabriolet is a rarely seen motor car and can be easily recognised by the fact that it is a 2-seater, with rear styling accordingly much more curvaceous than its Karmann counterpart. The hood on the Hebmüller is of a completely different fitment and, when in the lowered position, does not appear nearly as bulky. Another identification point of an early model Karmann is the distinctive 'Karmann Kabriolet' badge, lodged neatly onto the front quarterpanel.

The Karmann Cabriolet was designated Type 15 by Volkswagen and, when put into production initially, achieved very meagre build quantities. At first, only two cars per day were leaving Osnabrück between June 1949 (when production

A prototype
Beetle
with roll-
back roof
pictured
on test.
(Courtesy
Volkswagen)

A Car with a Difference –
but still a true Volkswagen

Cars of exclusive design are thought a risky buy because they may lack the backing of large scale trials and testing. There is no such risk, however, with the VW Convertible, for it offers you all the virtues and quality that have made the name of Volkswagen famous and sought after throughout the world. Almost two million Volkswagens have now been sold – a proof of their sturdiness and quality!

Engine	4-cylinder, 4-stroke, O. H. V. type, air-cooled, with horizontally opposed cylinders. Compression ratio 6.6 Bore 3.031 in., Displacement 72.740 cu.in. (1192 c. c.), Stroke 2.520 in., S. A. E. h. p. 36 at 3700 r. p. m.	*Chassis*	Tubular center section forked at rear with welded-on platform	*Fuel tank capacity*	10.6 U. S. gal. (8.75 Imp. gal., 40 liters) incl. 1.3 U. S. gal. (1.1 Imp. gal., 5 liters) reserve
		Front axle	Independent suspension of wheels through trailing arms, 2 laminated square-section torsion bars protected by tubes	*Dimensions*	Length 160.2 in. (4070 mm.), width 60.6 in. (1540 mm.), height 59.1 in. (1500 mm.)
Carburetor	Downdraft carburetor with acceleration pump	*Rear axle*	Independent suspension through swing-axle shafts, trailing arms and one round torsion bar on each side	*Weights*	Unladen weight 1764 lbs. (800 kg.), max. load 793 lbs. (360 kg.), max. total weight 2557 lbs. (1160 kg.)
Cooling system	Air cooling, fan-operated, automatically controlled by thermostat	*Shock absorbers*	Double-acting telescopic type	*Performance*	Fuel consumption according to DIN 70030 32 m. p. g. (U. S.), 39 m. p. g. (Imp.), 7.5 liters / 100 km. Max. and cruising speed 68 m. p. h. = 110 km./h. Climbing ability in 1st gear 18.5° (34%)
Lubrication	Pressure lubrication (gear-type pump) with oil cooler	*Tires*	Five tubeless, large-section super balloon tires, 5.60-15		
Transmission	Synchromesh on 2nd, 3rd and 4th gears	*Footbrake*	Hydraulic type (Lockheed), operating on 4 wheels		
Final drive	Power transmitted through spiral bevel gear and differential gear via two swing-axle shafts to rear wheels	*Wheelbase*	94.5 in. · Turning circle 36 ft. · Track front 50.8 in., rear 49.2 in.		

Outer mirror at extra cost

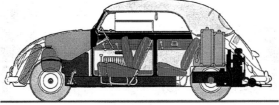

Seats situated in best sprung part between the axles affording plenty of leg and head room to all occupants. Adequate luggage space provided under front hood and behind rear seats. Rear-mounted engine for top performance and easy maintenance. Large fuel tank with reserve supply. Smooth silent synchromesh transmission. VW air cooling system — equally effective in arctic and tropical climates.

VOLKSWAGENWERK GMBH · WOLFSBURG · GERMANY

VW dubbed the Karmann Cabriolet 'A Car with a Difference' whilst seeking to reassure customers that it was still a true Volkswagen. (Courtesy National Motor Museum)

The Volkswagen chassis was popular with coachbuilders. The Rometsch, as shown here, earned the nickname 'The Banana' because of its curved shape. (Courtesy National Motor Museum)

Beetle Cabriolet variants such as the Rometsch, depicted here and photographed at Hessisch Oldendorf in 2009, are particularly sought-after. Compare the vehicle shown in this photograph with the tired-looking example depicted in the mono image above. (Courtesy Ken Cservenka)

commenced) and September 1949; by the end of the year this figure had increased threefold and six cars a day were passing through Karmann's factory. Four months into 1950, the 1000th car had been completed and a further 1695 built between then and the end of December.

As with the Karmann Ghia, the 4-seat Cabriolet was constructed upon the Export, otherwise known as the De Luxe, Beetle platform. In general, the mechanical specification changes made to the VW Beetle Export Saloon applied equally to the Cabriolet. Apart from body styling, the major difference between the two cars was weight, the Cabriolet being some 200lb (90kg) heavier. This was all due to the increased strengthening and extra box section girders that were essential to compensate for the lack of the steel roof and subsequent loss of torsional stiffness.

Continued on page 49

Although coachbuilt by Drews, this Cabriolet features the Beetle dashboard. (Author's collection)

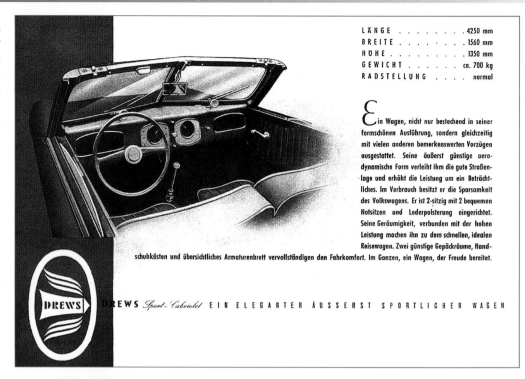

LÄNGE . . . . 4250 mm
BREITE . . . . 1560 mm
HÖHE . . . . 1350 mm
GEWICHT . . . . . . ca. 700 kg
RADSTELLUNG . . . . normal

Ein Wagen, nicht nur bestechend in seiner formschönen Ausführung, sondern gleichzeitig mit vielen anderen bemerkenswerten Vorzügen ausgestattet. Seine äußerst günstige aerodynamische Form verleiht ihm die gute Straßenlage und erhöht die Leistung um ein Beträchtliches. Im Verbrauch besitzt er die Sparsamkeit des Volkswagens. Er ist 2-sitzig mit 2 bequemen Notsitzen und Lederpolsterung eingerichtet. Seine Geräumigkeit, verbunden mit der hohen Leistung machen ihn zu dem schnellen, idealen Reisewagen. Zwei günstige Gepäckräume, Handschuhkästen und übersichtliches Armaturenbrett vervollständigen den Fahrkomfort. Im Ganzen, ein Wagen, der Freude bereitet.

DREWS *Sport-Cabriolet* EIN ELEGANTER ÄUSSERST SPORTLICHER WAGEN

The Karmann Cabriolet always attracted attention wherever it went. Note the round horn grille which identifies this as an early example. (Courtesy National Motor Museum)

Why does VW meet with universal admiration? Because its reliability and comfort is nearest to an ideal car. While many books have been written about the VW, this folder is intended only to outline briefly the outstanding features. A rear mounted engine, having two pairs of horizontally opposed cylinders • Phenomenal gas mileage of 37.5 miles per gallon at 34 m.p.h. • The cooling problem is successfully solved by the revolutionary automatically controlled air cooling system which eliminates radiator boiling, freezing or overheating, regardless of speed, load or hill climbing • Oil cooled by the air flow assures dependable engine lubrication even when

Convertible

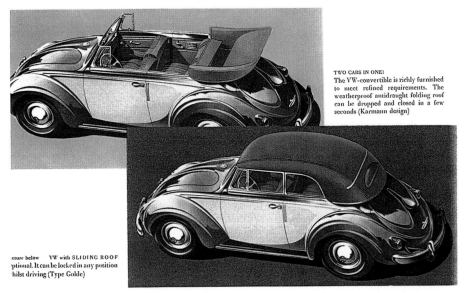

TWO CARS IN ONE!
The VW-convertible is richly furnished to meet refined requirements. The weatherproof antidraught folding roof can be dropped and closed in a few seconds (Karmann design)

cture below   VW with SLIDING ROOF
ptional. It can be locked in any position
hilst driving (Type Golde)

ar engine, with its superb automatically regulated air cooling system, ow piston speed and only 3000 RPM gives maximum life with great reserves of power. Acceleration and flexibility have been considerably mproved by the installation of a new downdraft carburettor with accelerator pump. The existing fine road-holding, a result of a low centre f gravity, equal weight distribution, superbly accurate finger-tip steering nd torsion bar suspension has been further improved by softer springing nd low pressure tyres. Following intense research work in the laboratory nd in the experimental field a really sound synchromesh transmission has been developed, with which gear changing is a pleasure. The interior nd exterior of the car have been tastefully modernized. These new features include effective sound insulation, better shaped and more luxurious seats, separate ventilation wings in the door windows, more efficient windshield wipers and a refined heating control. What remains unchanged, because it could not possibly be improved, is that perfect synthesis of performance and economy of the VW. Its low gasoline consumption and maintenance cost and its widespread service facilities have made the VW extremely popular. Its manoeuverability in city traffic and on winding country roads with its low running costs classify it as a "small car", but its speed, reliability and general performance elevate it far above itself. Truly the VW is a "class in itself"; a car to fill all demands; a great feat of ingenuity and engineering!

Sliding Roof

Volkswagen marketed the Cabriolet – or, as in this instance, the convertible – as 'Two Cars In One!' Open to the elements with the hood lowered, the car could be converted to a weatherproof, anti-draught saloon in a few seconds. The illustrations are typical of the Volkswagen marketing campaign of the period. (Courtesy Volkswagen)

Fahrgestell

(Limousine und Cabriolet)

Technische Daten

Federung vorn . . . 2 durchgehende Vierkant-Drehfederstäbe, querliegend

Federung hinten . . 1 runder Drehfederstab auf jeder Seite, querliegend

Stoßdämpfer . . . . vorn und hinten doppeltwirkende Teleskopstoßdämpfer

Lenkung . . . . . . VW-Spindel-Lenkung mit geteilter Spurstange

Lenkradumdrehungen von Anschlag zu Anschlag . 2,4

Kleinster Wendekreisdurchmesser . . etwa 11 m

Räder . . . . Scheibenräder mit Tiefbettfelge 4 J x 15

Bereifung . . . . 5,60—15

Luftdruck

Besetzung 1 bis 2 Personen . . vorn 1,1 atü; hinten 1,4 atü

Besetzung 3 bis 5 Personen . . vorn 1,2 atü; hinten 1,6 atü

Bremsen

Exportmodell und Cabriolet:

Fußbremse . . . Hydraulische Vierradbremse (Ate)

Handbremse . . Mechanisch, auf die Hinterräder wirkend

Standardmodell:

Fuß- und Handbremse . . Mechanische VW-Vierradbremse

Radstand . . . . 2400 mm

Spurweite . . . . vorn 1290 mm; hinten 1250 mm

Sturz . . . . 0° 40'

Vorspur (bei Leergewicht) . . 1 bis 3 mm

Nachlauf . . . . . 2° 30'

1 Lenkgetriebe
2 Vorderachse
3 Rahmenkopf
4 Spurstange
5 Hauptbremszylinder
6 Fußhebelwerk
7 Lenkrad
8 Schalthebel
9 Bodenblech
10 Handbremshebel
11 Drehgriff für Heizung
12 Rahmentunnel
13 Batterie
14 Hinteres Tragrohr mit Drehstäben
15 Triebling
16 Rahmengabel
17 Anlasser
18 Antriebswelle
19 Getriebegehäuse
20 Ausgleichgetriebe
21 Hinterachse
22 Kupplung
23 Nockenwelle
24 Kurbelwelle
25 Kühlgebläse
26 Auspuff
27 Lichtmaschine
28 Vergaser

The Volkswagen Beetle chassis was used as a basis for the Karmann Ghia. (Courtesy Stiftung AutoMuseum Volkswagen)

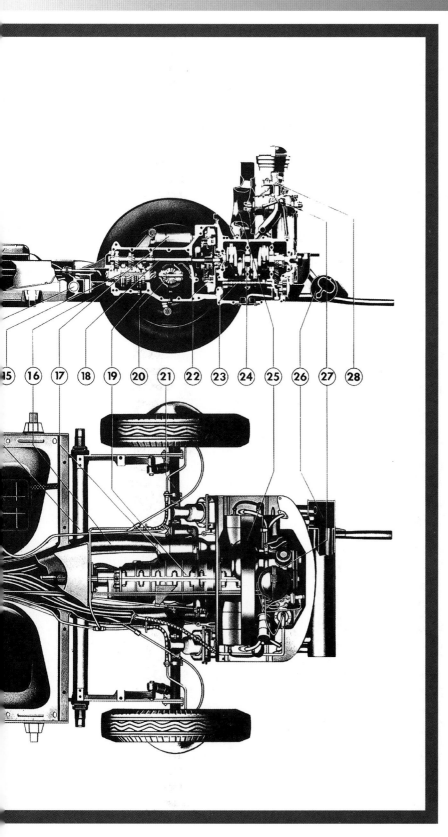

The desirability of the genuine Karmann Cabriolet has led, not surprisingly, to the appearance of a number of less successful conversions from standard Beetles into would-be dropheads. Apart from the non-original aspect, it's unlikely that these vehicles achieve the engineering integrity of the original, and in extreme cases, due to a disregard of structural essentials, could be a safety hazard.

There are usually tell-tale indications to whether a Cabriolet is authentic or not; Karmann-built Cabriolets have a higher waistline than Saloon cars, and the coachwork above the bright trim strip of the swage line is more detailed and better defined than would be the case on a Wolfsburg-built car.

Amongst the outstanding features of the Karmann Cabriolet is the quality of the hood, which is noted for its durability as well as being virtually draught-free and leak-proof. Not in any way a lightweight affair, the hood comprises three layers of material; a plastic headlining and vinyl outer covering sandwiching a concoction of rubberised fabric mixed with horsehair. The result was a heavy-duty, rugged hood which served to keep the car as warm, dry and comfortable as would the steel roof of a Saloon car.

To accompany the first Karmann Cabriolet, Volkswagen produced a delightful and specially prepared colour brochure. To emphasize the Cabrio styling, the illustration on the cover pictured the car from the three-quarter rear view, and the features of the car are clearly defined. The black-over-beige coachwork, stylized to even greater effect with black wings and body-coloured wheels, highlighted the external door hinges and front-mounted semaphores. Unique are the air-intake louvres on the engine compartment lid and the narrow rear window built into the hood. The familiar, characteristic split oval rear window found on the early Saloon cars was never a feature of the Cabriolet.

It was by necessity that the air-intakes on the Cabriolet were designed quite differently to those of the Volkswagen Beetle Saloon, which

Das Fahrgestell

hat einen durch Stahlbleche abgedeckten, drehungssteifen Mittelrahmen mit einer rückwärtigen Gabelung zur Aufnahme der Antriebsaggregate: Motor, Kupplung, Getriebe, Differential - und der Hinterachse. Reserverad und Tank sind auf dem Rahmenkopf angebracht.

Der Motor

Der KdF-Wagen hat einen gegenläufigen Vierzylinder-Motor, der im Heck des Wagens untergebracht ist. Die Zylinder arbeiten im Viertakt und haben einen Hubraum von 986 ccm. Der Motor leistet 23,5 PS bei der normalen Drehzahl von 3000 pro Minute; das entspricht einer Stundengeschwindigkeit von rund 100 km.

Publicity pictures of the chassis of the original Volkswagen. (Courtesy Stiftung AutoMuseum Volkswagen)

were situated below the split oval window and above the engine cover. Due to the positioning of the Cabriolet's hood, which extended almost as far as the engine hatch, the louvres were re-designed in shape and punched into the lid itself. This, however, did not allow adequate air to circulate the engine when the hood was lowered. Whilst not too much of a concern when driving at slower speeds and taking shorter journeys, the engine tended to run at higher than optimum temperatures over longer distances, and especially at higher speeds.

Early modifications

Some of the design alterations, such as semaphore positioning and style of door hinge, have already been detailed. Saloon cars were fitted with an opening vent to allow fresh air to enter the car through the front quarterpanel, and this device was also provided for the Cabriolet, but only for a year. The

ventilator flap proved unpopular, as it created a cold, hurricane-like draught that blew onto driver's and passenger's feet and legs once the car was on the move. The same could be said for the little Fiat Topolino, which employed an almost identical system. On the Cabriolet, fitment of the ventilator had been made possible by re-positioning the semaphore signals on the rear quarterpanels. This modification was soon replaced by swivelling quarterlights in the front windows which controlled airflow far more efficiently.

Below each of the headlights appeared a horn grille, initially circular in shape but changing to an oval design after October 1952. The grille on the left-hand side of the car was the real thing, the matching grille on the right was purely ornamental to balance the appearance of the car. As for the headlamp

Continued on page 55

The engine compartment as featured in the original KdF Wagen brochure. (Courtesy Volkswagen/ Author's collection)

DER MOTOR DES KDF=WAGENS

Der KdF=Wagen hat einen Vierzylinder=Boxermotor, der im Heck des Wagens untergebracht ist. Die Zylinder arbeiten im Viertakt und haben einen Hubraum von 986 ccm. Bei einer normalen Drehzahl von 3000 p. M. leistet der Wagen 23,5 PS, das entspricht einer Stundengeschwindigkeit von rund 100 km.

Der Motor hat Luftkühlung. Im Luftführungsgehäuse ist der Ölkühler untergebracht, der so bemessen ist, daß niedrige Öltemperaturen auch bei größter Beanspruchung stets für eine ausreichende Schmierung aller Schmierstellen des Motors sorgen. Hierdurch wird die erstaunliche Autobahnfestig= keit des KdF=Wagens erreicht, die Höchstgeschwindigkeit gleich Dauergeschwindigkeit sein läßt. Die Kühlung wird n i c h t wie bei einem vorn liegenden Motor von der Geschwindigkeit des Fahrzeuges beeinflußt, sondern hängt von der Drehzahl des Motors ab. Dadurch wird in gebirgigem Gelände selbst bei geringer Geschwindigkeit und höchster Motorbeanspruchung eine Überhitzung restlos vermieden.

Ventile:	kopfgesteuert.
Zündung:	Batterie=Lichtmaschinenzündung.
Batterie:	6 Volt.
Lichtmaschine:	spannungsregulierend.
Anlasser:	mit Ritzel auf Schwungrad wirkend.
Vergaser:	Fallstromvergaser.

8

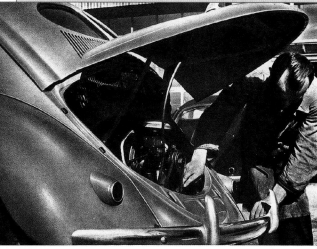

Der Motor im Heck des KdF-Wagens ist gut zugänglich

Kraftstoff=Förderung:	entsprechend den bestehenden Vorschriften sind Motor und Benzintank von= einander getrennt untergebracht. Eine Kraftstoffpumpe fördert das Benzin vom Tank zum Motor.
Kupplung:	Einscheibentrockenkupplung.
Getriebe:	4 Vorwärtsgänge, 1 Rückwärtsgang, 3. und 4. Gang geräuscharm. Die Höchstgeschwindigkeit des 1. Ganges ist 20 km, des 2. Ganges 40 km, des 3. Ganges 65 km in der Stunde.
Ölverbrauch:	normal nur bei Ölwechsel (2,5 Liter für etwa 2500 Kilometer).
Kraftstoff=Verbrauch:	6 bis 7 Liter Benzin auf 100 Kilometer je nach Fahrweise und Gelände.

Der Motor des KdF=Wagens zeichnet sich durch leichte Zugänglichkeit zu seinen Einzelteilen aus, der Motoraus= und =einbau ist in kürzester Frist durchzuführen, man braucht dazu etwa je 10 Min. Der Motor des KdF=Wagens ist so konstruiert, daß alle Sorten Benzin des In= und Auslandes gefahren werden können.

Und die Reparaturen?
Es werden neuartige Wege beschritten werden, die Ausgaben für Reparaturen, wenn sie notwendig werden sollten, so niedrig wie möglich zu halten. Eine Vereinfachung ist schon dadurch gegeben, daß die einzelnen Teile des KdF-Wagens, auch der Motor, gut zugänglich sind und ebenso leicht montiert werden können. Ferner werden eine ganze Reihe Austauschteile vor= bereitet. Bei größeren Unfällen tritt die Versicherung in Kraft.

9

Final checks before leaving the factory. An original picture from KdF Wagen publicity. (Courtesy Volkswagen/Author's collection)

This early Cabriolet depicts models known within VW circles as the 'Split Era.' It dates from before October 1952, as after that date, Cabriolets were given oval instead of round horn grilles, and headlamps were of Volkswagen build instead of the later Bosch type. (Courtesy Ken Cservenka)

Interior of the 'Split Era' Cabriolet showing, in this case, a nice patina which is in keeping with a well-used and maintained car. Being of pre-October 1952 build, it has the early facia with twin instruments which, after that date, was redesigned with a single dial. (Courtesy Ken Cservenka)

The Cabrio's air intake louvres were quite different to those of the Beetle saloon. (Courtesy Martin McGarry)

Depicting what is termed the 'Oval Era' in Beetle Cabriolet chronology is this USA-specification example. The horn grilles are oval instead of the earlier round type, and note the bullet indicators. Finishing off this cared-for car are the whitewall tyres. (Courtesy Ken Cservenka)

CONVERTIBLE

Both the De Luxe Saloon (also available with sun roof) and the luxurious Volkswagen Convertible offer the same typical features that distinguish every Volkswagen:
classic and timeless body design;
the Volkswagen air-cooled flat four engine;
Volkswagen torsion-bar springing.
Is driving an open car in fresh air and sunlight your sport? Do you want a car that underlines your individuality? If so, you will enjoy the Volkswagen Convertible. Every lady who takes the wheel is enchanted with the restrained beauty of this smart convertible, with its graceful lines and its first class driving qualities, so typical of the VW. The Volkswagen Convertible is economical, yet eager to go. It handles effortlessly, whether in the thick of traffic or on hairpin mountain bends. With its broad spectrum of truly distinguished shades, the range of standard colours for convertibles and saloons pleases any taste. The brilliance and superb quality of the enamel endow the VW with lasting value. Volkswagen owners the world over park their cars outdoors without a qualm — the triple armour of enamel is their garage.

Parking with a smile! There's always room to slip in with a Volkswagen — the perfection of agility and easy handling.

Ernst Reuters' illustrative material for Volkswagen is recognised as an artform, and his drawings of the Beetle Convertible shown here are as attractive now as they were in the early- to mid-1950s. Volkswagen's marketing message is clearly directed at lady drivers, who would, it was claimed, be enchanted by the restrained beauty of the smart Convertible, with its graceful lines and first-class driving qualities. Selling motor cars to women was a lucrative market in America at the time. In the UK it was a different matter, with the country struggling to free itself from postwar austerity. (Courtesy Volkswagen)

units, the originals – manufactured solely by Volkswagen – were discarded in favour of those made by Bosch.

Inside the Cabriolet there were significant changes: the upholstery was made even more comfortable, although rear passengers lost the luxury of elegant side bolster cushions; the dashboard, characteristic of the early Beetle, was soon to lose its twin dials in their distinctive housings, and was re-equipped with the more functional, if less appealing, single dial. The new facia design proved more functional than the original, and incorporated a radio housing as well as a lockable glovebox. Mechanically, the Beetle Cabriolet received the same modifications as the Export model Beetle, one of the most important being upgrading the braking system from cable operation to hydraulic. For the sake of convenience, the brake fluid reservoir was installed in the front luggage compartment, a position barely accessible as it was virtually underneath the fuel tank.

Having been specified from April 1950, the hydraulic braking system received its first modification only a month later, when the master cylinder and rear wheel brake cylinders were reduced slightly in size: less than 3mm at the front and a little over 3mm at the rear. The drum brakes were practically identical for both the front and rear wheels, with leading and trailing shoes incorporated in each drum. The handbrake mechanism operated on the rear wheels.

The suspension on early models also underwent modification and was made somewhat firmer by the addition of extra torsion springs, five springs being contained in each of the axle tubes. Less than eighteen months later, in April 1951, telescopic shock absorbers replaced the original lever type on the rear suspension. It would seem that Volkswagen was concerned about the suspension design as a whole because, after another eighteen months, in October 1952, the torsion leaf springs were again uprated and six springs per tube instead of five were specified.

By the end of 1952 a multitude of modifications had been implemented since the Cabriolet's introduction, many of which appeared outwardly insignificant. The engine remained largely unaltered but specification changes were made to the carburation and transmission. Early Karmann Cabriolets were prone to flatspots, the cause of which was eventually traced to the design of carburettor, which had relatively poor mixture control capabilities. To rectify this problem Volkswagen specified

The VOLKSWAGEN, Convertible

The Cabriolet underwent several changes in its early years; this model dates from 1951, as indicated by the ventilation flap on the front quarterpanel. This feature lasted for a year before opening quarterlights were added to the front windows. Note that the semaphores are installed in the rear quarterpanels.
(Courtesy National Motor Museum)

THE SUNROOF

Many who like driving in an open car, but do not want a convertible, find the ideal solution in the Volkswagen Sunroof which is an optional extra on both the Custom and DeLuxe models. When closed, the flexible folding roof is draft-free, snow and rain-proof. In winter the Volkswagen Sunroof is as snug as a closed car.

In addition to the Cabrio, the 'Sunroof' model was also available. (Courtesy National Motor Museum)

THE CONVERTIBLE

Here is the utmost in convertible smartness . . . a truly distinctive car with a thickly padded, sound and weather insulating top that can be opened or closed in seconds. The interior appointments, upholstery and general coachwork of finest German craftsmanship will appeal to the most discriminating.

Easy to Park The exceptional manoeuvrability of the Volkswagen is a boon to city drivers (and to the ladies too!). It will park easily in the smallest space.

Curb-line-vision "Curb-line-vision" gives a complete view of the road, an important factor for safer driving, made possible by mounting the engine in the rear.

Among early modifications was the introduction of tail lights with upward-facing lenses:
a feature from late 1952. (Courtesy National Motor Museum)

the use of the Solex 28 PCI carburettor, which was fitted with both an accelerator pump and pump jet; the result was totally better performance, with none of the previous problems. As for the transmission, the 'crash' gearbox was superseded by a modified version which employed cone-type synchromesh on 2nd, 3rd and 4th ratios. However, the 'crash' box lived on in its standard version in the Beetle Saloon for some time.

From October 1952, the Cabriolet, as well as the Beetle built at Wolfsburg, received slightly smaller diameter wheels; instead of 5.60x16, 5.60x15 wheels were fitted, complete with crossply tyres. Today, however, Cabrio and Beetle owners usually fit radial ply tyres in place of crossplys, because they give improved performance and handling.

Cosmetically, late 1952 cars can be identified by revised tail lights which had lenses for the brake lights built into the upper part of the lamp pod. This was instead of the single brake lamp being housed within what was commonly referred to as the 'Pope's Nose,' which was centrally mounted upon the engine cover. The Pope's Nose was modified to act as a registration plate lamp and was thus slightly re-shaped. A criticism of the new-style tail and brake lights is that they were very difficult to see, even at night. Despite being ineffectual, the skyward-pointing rear lamps remained for three years, until 1955.

At the end of 1953 there were two extremely significant changes to specification: a more powerful engine and a further modification to the suspension. Due to the end-of-year date for implementing the new engine, it's generally considered that this was designed for the 1954 model year. However, at this period in Volkswagen history, the model year started in January and extended through to December. The number of cars, Saloons and Cabriolets, fitted with the modified engine for the 1953 model year was, therefore, very small. It wasn't until 1955 that the model year was re-structured from August to August, so as to coincide with the annual factory shutdown.

The 1131cc motor had performed admirably in some half-million Beetles, not counting the Type 2 Transporters. Whilst this engine had provided perfectly acceptable performance in its earlier years, the faithful 25bhp unit was considered underpowered in an age when manufacturers were striving for more and more performance. Luckily, the more powerful – by just 5bhp – new 1192cc boxer engine was also made available for the Karmann Ghia when launched in 1955. Top speed of the Cabriolet rose from a lethargic amble of barely 60mph (96km/h) to a more vigorous 68mph (109km/h). The better performance was also due to the increased compression ratio, raised to 6.1:1 from 5.8:1; a further increase to 6.6:1 was augmented a few months later, in August 1954. To complement the more powerful engine, Volkswagen found it necessary to increase the size of the four inlet valves from 28.6mm diameter to 30mm, whilst a redesigned distributor boosted overall performance. A

more powerful dynamo, 160w instead of 130w, ensured more efficient use of the battery.

Yet another modification in the suspension design, implemented in a further attempt to improve ride comfort, resulted in the front torsion bars being uprated with the addition of two extra leaves, making a total of eight. The brake reservoir was moved from its rather cramped position beneath the fuel tank, to the front apron behind the spare wheel, where it was much more accessible.

In an attempt to comply with legislation in countries where the Karmann Cabriolet was marketed, certain technical improvements had to be made to the car's specification. Often, such specification changes were implemented for export vehicles ahead of the cars destined for the home market, as with the design of the rear lights which, for the USA, were changed for double filament types in 1954, allowing both tail and brake lights to be incorporated within a single lens. It was a further two years before this modification was made available for the European market.

By the end of 1954 production of the Karmann Cabriolet amounted to over 20,000 vehicles; in the five years of manufacture a fraction over 1000 cars had been exported to the USA. However, from 1955 on, when Volkswagen's American headquarters was set up in New York, exportation of cars across the Atlantic intensified dramatically.

Production increases

In 1955, for the first time, production of the Karmann Cabriolet rose above 6000 cars per annum. In fact, until 1954, when 4740 Cabriolets were built, production had not totalled 5000 cars in any one year. For 1955, therefore, it was seen as evidence of a massive boost in the model's popularity that 6000 cars left Osnabrück.

1955 was altogether an auspicious year for both Volkswagen and the German motor industry. Not only were sales of the ubiquitous Beetle generally growing at a fast rate, in what was the 10th year of its postwar production, but the one millionth Beetle was built on August 5th that year.

Cabriolets bound for America during 1955 underwent a number of design modifications which had not, at that time, been specified for European production. Possibly the most important was the replacement of semaphore signal direction indicators with flashing indicators, which were incorporated in clear lenses on the sides of the front wings. Whilst many British and European car manufacturers had already chosen to employ flashing direction indicators, Volkswagen remained loyal to semaphores for a further five years, until 1960. Another significant modification was to the bumper, which received

Continued on page 60

THE VISIBLE INTERIOR

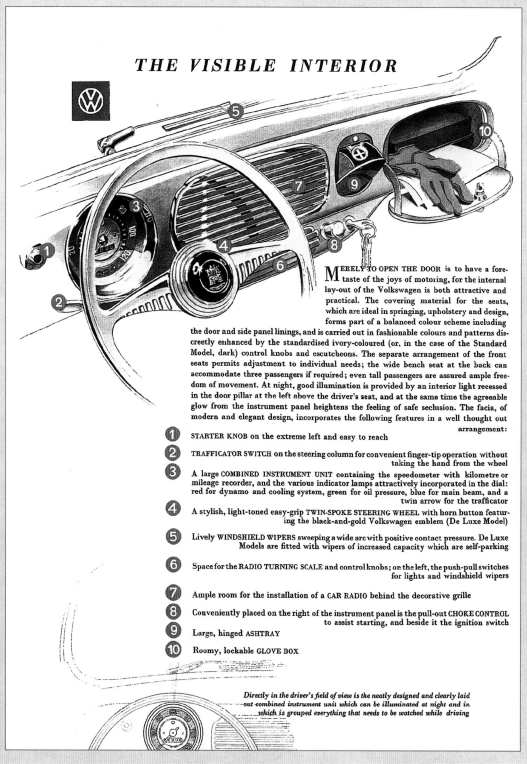

MERELY TO OPEN THE DOOR is to have a foretaste of the joys of motoring, for the internal
lay-out of the Volkswagen is both attractive and
practical. The covering material for the seats,
which are ideal in springing, upholstery and design,
forms part of a balanced colour scheme including
the door and side panel linings, and is carried out in fashionable colours and patterns discreetly enhanced by the standardised ivory-coloured (or, in the case of the Standard
Model, dark) control knobs and escutcheons. The separate arrangement of the front
seats permits adjustment to individual needs; the wide bench seat at the back can
accommodate three passengers if required; even tall passengers are assured ample freedom of movement. At night, good illumination is provided by an interior light recessed
in the door pillar at the left above the driver's seat, and at the same time the agreeable
glow from the instrument panel heightens the feeling of safe seclusion. The facia, of
modern and elegant design, incorporates the following features in a well thought out
arrangement:

① STARTER KNOB on the extreme left and easy to reach

② TRAFFICATOR SWITCH on the steering column for convenient finger-tip operation without
taking the hand from the wheel

③ A large COMBINED INSTRUMENT UNIT containing the speedometer with kilometre or
mileage recorder, and the various indicator lamps attractively incorporated in the dial:
red for dynamo and cooling system, green for oil pressure, blue for main beam, and a
twin arrow for the trafficator

④ A stylish, light-toned easy-grip TWIN-SPOKE STEERING WHEEL with horn button featur-
ing the black-and-gold Volkswagen emblem (De Luxe Model)

⑤ Lively WINDSHIELD WIPERS sweeping a wide arc with positive contact pressure. De Luxe
Models are fitted with wipers of increased capacity which are self-parking

⑥ Space for the RADIO TURNING SCALE and control knobs; on the left, the push-pull switches
for lights and windshield wipers

⑦ Ample room for the installation of a CAR RADIO behind the decorative grille

⑧ Conveniently placed on the right of the instrument panel is the pull-out CHOKE CONTROL
to assist starting, and beside it the ignition switch

⑨ Large, hinged ASHTRAY

⑩ Roomy, lockable GLOVE BOX

*Directly in the driver's field of view is the neatly designed and clearly laid
out combined instrument unit which can be illuminated at night and in
which is grouped everything that needs to be watched while driving*

From October 1952 the Cabriolet – along with the Beetle – was treated to a revised
dashboard arrangement. This page from a sales brochure extols the virtues of the
dashboard modifications. (Courtesy National Motor Museum)

Above left: Karmann craftsmen employed on the Beetle Cabriolet striving to achieve perfection. The high standards at Osnabrück was unquestionable. (Karmann publicity/Author's collection)

Above: A busy scene at the Osnabrück trim shop, where only the finest materials were used. (Karmann publicity/Author's collection)

Left: Inside Karmann's factory. The lack of large presses resulted in labour-intensive assembly of many small body panels. The extent of the works is obvious, as is output with three assembly lines. (Karmann publicity/Author's collection)

With the arrival of flashing indicators the rear quarterpanels were revised. (Courtesy Martin McGarry)

taller overriders and an additional bar above the main blade at the front. At the rear the bumper was also double-bladed which gave protection to the lamps; the shape of the top bar was such that it did not obstruct the opening of the engine compartment lid. This design was also found on the Karmann Ghia, albeit with modifications to suit the car's styling.

During the mid-fifties, much of Volkswagen's production effort went into building enough cars to keep abreast of demand; so it was with the Karmann Cabriolet which, year by year, maintained a progressive increase in production. Some modifications were of a mechanical nature, in line with those of the export model Saloons. Tubeless tyres were obviously a major advantage to the Cabriolet's performance and cars were so supplied, after an initial trial which involved some 800 Beetle Saloons, from the middle of July 1956.

Mainly of interest to enthusiasts concerned with the restoration of early model Cabriolets is the fact that the material for the hood retaining studs was changed from steel to rust-resistant brass during 1956.

Due to the Cabriolet's popularity, and in an effort to produce as many cars as possible, modifications were kept to

a minimum during the mid-1950s, and only those considered essential were specified. However, this policy changed quite dramatically in 1957 because a host of changes were announced which considerably affected the Karmann-built Cabriolet. The changes were, in fact, intended for the 1958 model year as, by that time, Wolfsburg was completely geared to producing the new season's models from August, to correspond with the factory's annual shutdown.

Changes to the Cabriolet were, to a large extent, the result of far-reaching design alterations to the Beetle Saloon; apart from losing its charming oval rear window to one of a more rectangular shape, the Beetle's front window was also enlarged. The Cabriolet, too, received a larger expanse of glass at the rear, which enhanced rearward visibility and allowed more light into the car's interior. The bigger windscreen was the direct result of modifications to the Beetle, which was given appreciably slimmer A-posts.

If the larger front and rear windscreens didn't entirely identify the Cabriolet as being a post-1957 car, then the shape of the air inlets on the engine compartment cover did. Instead of having vertically-shaped louvres as previously, post-1957 cars

Rear lights were also modified on post-1961 models. (Courtesy Martin McGarry)

had two sets of horizontal slats, five on each side, punched into the engine lid. A further point of identification is the design of the engine cover, which lost, to a great extent, the exaggerated 'W' moulding.

Apart from exterior styling differences, 1957/8 cars were given a face-lifted dashboard, only the second such change in the history of the Karmann Cabriolet. A push-button radio was provided in the centre of the facia, taking the place of the speaker grille previously there, which was relocated to the left-hand side of the speedometer on left-hand drive cars, and to the right on cars with right-hand drive. Between the radio and speedometer, a dummy speaker grille was added for cosmetic purposes.

The layout of the controls was also altered: the switches for the headlights and windscreen wipers were placed towards the top of the facia, and the ignition switch moved nearer to the driver instead of being virtually in front of the passenger seat. Although the direction indicator switch controlling the semaphores – by now considered old-fashioned and a safety hazard since flashing signals had become common – was attached to the steering column, the device was intended to self-cancel. The rather neat ashtray, built vertically into the facia, was, sadly, lost due to the arrival of a larger glovebox, which was considerably more useful than the previous type. The ashtray was re-housed below the facia and underneath the radio housing console; in its new position, this push/pull affair seemed never to work quite as efficiently as the old design and certainly was not as attractive.

Until this general face-lift, drivers were accustomed to operating the notoriously difficult and poorly positioned

The interior of a 1963 car. Note the wind-down rear quarter windows. (Courtesy Martin McGarry)

accelerator pedal – in reality, little more than a roller-ball. Now, mechanical modifications resulted in the provision of a proper accelerator pedal, which resembled a flat organ pedal.

Few design changes affected the Cabriolet from 1957/8 until the announcement of the 1960 model range, in the late summer of 1959. Possibly the most substantial modification was the addition of anti-roll bars to the front and rear suspension, which were designed to improve handling and performance. The modification had been incorporated in the front suspension of the Karmann Ghia from the outset of that car's production, in 1955. Specified from August 1959, the anti-roll bars reduced by a considerable extent a tendency to oversteer, an inherent trademark of the Beetle since introduction. A certain amount of criticism had been voiced about the Beetle's handling, which had a habit of catching out those drivers not used to the car's tail-happy attitude. Experienced Volkswagen owners may, however, have felt this rebuke somewhat unwarranted and actually preferred the Beetle as it was. There is some evidence that, in competitive motorsport, participants went as far as

removing the bars in order to increase the car's agility, enabling them to flip the car's rear end in and out of corners at speed.

For the new decade the Cabriolet underwent substantial changes, both cosmetically and mechanically. The most important mechanical development was the arrival of the 34bhp engine, still rated at 1192cc displacement, but with 4bhp more power. The new engine (previously installed in the Volkswagen Type 2 Transporter) was available from July 1960, which meant it was, in fact, intended for the 1961 model year. Together with the more powerful engine arrived a different carburettor, the Solex 28 PICT (with automatic choke), replacing the previously specified Solex 28 PCI unit. Whilst the 34bhp engine and uprated carburettor obviously improved performance beyond all measure, there was, understandably, a downside, inasmuch that fuel consumption was bound to suffer. All was not lost, though, as Volkswagen, from July onwards, fitted a modified gearbox with synchromesh on all four forward ratios.

Post-1961 model cars can normally be very easily identified by the flashing indicators positioned on the top of the front

Pictured with hood raised, this Cabrio dates from the mid-1960s, identified as such by the ventilated road wheels. (Courtesy Martin McGarry)

wings. Housed in chromium-plated, pendant-shaped units, the front indicators were fitted with an amber-coloured lens; at the rear the flashing indicators were incorporated within the existing tail light pods, which were furnished with red lens covers. The design of the rear lamp units was similar to that found on cars such as the Morris Minor, as well as a number of other vehicles of that period, where the red lens was used for tail, stop and turn functions. Amber rear indicators for the Cabriolet would have to wait a further year.

The demise of semaphores in favour of flashing turn indicators brought about the re-modelling of the Cabriolet's rear quarterpanels, resulting in an altogether smoother appearance. There were a number of other improvements, too: the fusebox, which hitherto had been located under the front bonnet in the luggage compartment, was repositioned inside the cabin and concealed with a plastic cover under the dashboard; shock absorbers provided a softer ride, whilst the addition of a steering damper improved the Cabriolet's handling and performance qualities.

Throughout 1961 – and more generally available for cars produced for the 1962 model year – a number of minor improvements increased the Cabriolet's driver appeal. The seats were given a greater amount of fore and aft movement, improving comfort for both tall and short drivers, and safety harness anchorages were provided but, as in the case of the Karmann Ghia, seat belts were not included as standard equipment and owners had to provide the belts themselves. Long overdue, however, was the installation of a factory-fitted fuel gauge, which rendered obsolete the reserve tap attached

to the fuel supply. Heating was also improved by modification to the outlet vents in the front footwells, and sliding covers enabled adjustment of the amount of heat entering the cabin at these points; by shutting the vents completely it was possible to direct an extra stream of warm air at the windscreen.

Mechanical modifications introduced to the chassis and running gear during 1961 were no less significant. Included was the provision of maintenance-free tie rods, as well as the introduction of a new type of steering box of the worm and roller type, instead of the worm and peg unit of previously. Possibly a minor point was the utilisation of spring-loaded front bonnet stays in preference to the sliding rod type; the original supports retained the bonnet in an open position by a spring clamp and the unsuspecting could easily try to close it without first releasing the clip – with disastrous results! Further changes to specification included lowering the temperature at which the thermostatic air-cooling regulator operated, from between 75-80 degrees C to 65-70 degrees C, and a marginal adjustment to the thickness of the inner spacer ring on the rear wheel bearings.

Relatively minor adjustments to the Cabriolet's specification continued throughout 1962 and 1963; a similar modification to the heating vents at the front of the cabin was applied to the rear compartment from the end of 1962 and, in early 1963, a new clutch cable – shortened by 10mm – was used. It was not until the autumn of 1963, in readiness for the 1964 season cars, that a number of cosmetic changes were introduced which included enlargement of the wing-mounted flashing indicators and re-shaping of the registration lamp pod on the engine cover.

Outstanding for 1964, although introduced after the annual summer factory closure, was re-shaping the Cabriolet's windscreen to incorporate a slight curvature, in order to provide improved forward visibility. This had been made possible by gentle re-structuring of the A-posts to make them somewhat slimmer. The construction of the Cabriolet, compared to the Saloon version of the Beetle, resulted in a slightly different profile for the front quarterlight frames; the style of those found on the Beetle were slightly raked on the uprights, and so appeared sleeker. By contrast, the quarterlights on the Cabriolet were of necessity rather squared-off, in order to be load-bearing, and emphasized the car's chunkier styling features round the waistline. Ventilation in the closed Cabriolet was never the same problem as it was in the Saloon, by virtue of the Cabriolet's wind-down rear windows. 1964 was also notable for the introduction of redesigned heating and ventilation controls, which did away with the familiar rotary knob adjacent to the gearshift; twin levers, one for the front and the other the rear, were fitted in the same way as those on the Karmann Ghia.

A new generation of cabriolets

By the mid-sixties the Beetle, along with the Cabriolet, was suffering a mid-life crisis. The problem was nothing to do with styling or ethos, but more about performance, or lack of it. Compared to other cars the Beetle was showing its age by lacking in acceleration and a respectable top speed, the two combining as a serious underpower – enough to induce a dip in the cars' popularity stakes. In addressing the performance issue, Wolfsburg engineers instigated a programme of engine development to restore the Volkswagen's position as one of the most sought-after cars.

To improve the Cabriolet's performance the 1300 engine used in the Karmann Ghia was specified. Not entirely new, the 1300 was a hybrid which had been produced by mating the crankshaft from the Type 3 Volkswagen engine with the crankcase from that of the old 1200 engine. With a capacity of 1285cc and an additional 6bhp – producing 40bhp in total – the power increase amounted to something approaching 17.5 per cent more than that of the original engine. Even with the Cabriolet's more muscular engine, which was eagerly welcomed by Volkswagen enthusiasts everywhere, the difference in performance was hardly spectacular, especially when similarly-sized cars from rival European manufacturers were striding ahead in performance terms.

For the majority of Volkswagen enthusiasts there was nothing to rival the Cabriolet, or for that matter, the Beetle. Another hand-built car offering such quality and reliability was simply not available. The new engine did at least mean that the car's top speed was also its cruising speed, something that Volkswagen often reminded its customers. Volkswagen claimed a maximum speed of 76mph (121.6km/h) and a 0-60mph (0-96km/h) acceleration of 23 seconds for the Cabriolet, though generally most road test results showed a figure nearer to 80mph (128km/h).

Some observers might have hoped that Volkswagen had taken a lead from some of the main tuning specialists, such as Okrasa, and modified the 1300 engine to incorporate a twin-port conversion. The conservatively-biased Volkswagen company nonetheless resisted such suggestions and remained loyal to its traditional principle of steady reliability.

Identification of the 1300 Karmann Cabriolet was made all the more obvious by its ventilated road wheels and a flatter design of hub cap, the latter replacing the familiar domed type. Inside the cabin, a modification to the heating and ventilation system (a further vent at the top of the dashboard) enabled more air to be directed at the windscreen. As a driving aid, the headlamp dip-switch was moved from its foot-operated position on the floor, to the steering column, where it was far easier to use. The steering wheel received a semi-circular ring horn-push, whilst safety features included heavier duty seat mountings and a seat frame lock which prevented it sliding forwards in the event of an accident. Anti-burst locks were specified for the doors, which prevented them from flying open; particularly likely if the car was involved in a collision.

Changes to the chassis specification resulted in uprating the front suspension, which received two additional torsion leaves, making ten in total. The brake drums featured a ribbed pattern to enable better stopping distances, as well as preventing a build-up of latent heat which reduced overall efficiency. The steering mechanism was also modified to include ball joints, instead of king pins and link pin, whilst, at the front of the car, the wheel bearings were changed to the tapered roller type.

1967 and 1968 were important years for the Karmann Cabriolet, though for different reasons. Cars produced for the 1967 model year were fitted with an engine with even greater output than that of the 1300 introduced for the previous year; vehicles designated for 1968, however, and produced from August 1967 onwards, were given a startling face-lift which was in some danger of changing the whole styling concept of the car.

However excellent the Karmann Cabriolet was judged to be, in the late '60s it still experienced a drop in sales figures. As a result, production dipped significantly from something approaching 11,000 units in 1965, to a little over 7500 units for 1967, a fall, thereabouts, of 30%. On the other hand, in 1971 production rapidly increased from this low point to peak at over 24,000 vehicles.

Much of the Karmann's new-found popularity that year was undoubtedly due to the availability of the 1500 engine, which was very much akin to that found in the Type 3 Volkswagen.

This early seventies car illustrates the changes made – as a result of US legislation – to headlamp and wing assemblies, in August 1967. (Courtesy Martin McGarry)

European wing-top indicators were of a different design to those fitted to USA specification cars. Compare the design of this indicator housing adorning a 1303 Cabriolet to that shown in the previous photograph. (Courtesy Ken Cservenka)

Possibly the earliest surviving British-registered Beetle saloon parades in front of a number of Volkswagens, including a couple of Cabriolets. (Courtesy National Motor Museum)

Had not Volkswagen's plans for a 4-seat Type 3 Convertible fallen from favour due to its lack of torsional body strength, the Karmann Beetle Cabriolet's popularity would surely have suffered and the car, at worst, have faded into obscurity. The fact that the Type 3 Convertible did not materialise was the Beetle Cabriolet's saving grace.

Improvements contiguous with the adoption of the 1500 engine were numerous: front disc brakes were specified, together with dual circuits and a front anti-roll bar (drum brakes were retained at the rear). In order to give the car greater stability – and there were those who considered the car stable enough already – the rear track was not only widened, but the suspension provided with the benefit of an equalising spring connecting the rear torsion bars each side of the car.

The 1500 engine, with a capacity of 1493cc, produced 44bhp at 4000rpm, which was considered rather dynamic when compared with the original cars, and pushed the maximum speed upwards of 80mph (128km/h). Open the engine compartment lid and the bigger engine is very much evident by its re-designed air filter, which comprises two air feeds instead of the usual single affair. The carburettor used was the Solex 30 PICT I, and the engine number, stamped on the crankcase, had an 'H' prefix.

Although the 1500 was introduced in Europe with 6-volt electrics, the cars destined for America were supplied with a 12-volt system. American market cars were also provided with a re-designed engine cover, more upright in shape and with a slight bulge, not in order to house the larger engine

Larger rear lamps and four banks of air inlets are features of this late model Cabriolet.
(Courtesy Martin McGarry)

satisfactorily, as many people thought, but to comply with local legislation which demanded the registration plate be placed at a particular angle.

The host of lesser modifications included uprating the fuse box to contain ten fuses instead of eight; two-speed windscreen wipers, and a revised starter motor. The gearbox didn't escape alteration, either, and received a newly-designed case.

Design changes for cars produced for August 1967 went some way further. Most noticeable of the cosmetic alterations was the shape of the leading edge of the front wings, which resulted in restyling of the headlamps. Instead of following the shape of the sloping wing as previously, the revised lamps were more upright in response to American safety standards specifications. New bumpers were also to be found, and these were thicker in section as well as being considerably more robust; they were positioned higher than previously, which

meant that both the front boot lid and the engine cover had to be reduced in length. To accommodate the new design, the front and rear valances had to be re-shaped so as to be longer, and the bumper supports re-positioned.

These far-reaching design changes had a number of repercussions: the enlarged rear lamp units allowed reversing lamps to be incorporated within the light units as an optional extra; at the front of the car, the familiar horn grilles disappeared. The new styling incorporated an opening flap on the offside front quarterpanel, providing direct access to the neck of the petrol tank, and thereby dispensing with the need to open the bonnet when refuelling.

The styling face-lift was not only concerned with the car's exterior. The dashboard didn't escape attention and a re-designed speedometer, which incorporated the fuel gauge, replaced the earlier separate instruments. The ignition switch, instead

Curved windscreen and large section bumpers are evident on this late Karmann Cabriolet.
(Courtesy Martin McGarry)

of being housed in the middle of the facia, was positioned on the steering column; control switches were function-marked with standardised symbols and, for safety reasons, fabricated from soft plastic.

Notable for 1968 models was the change from a colour co-ordinated running board covering to a black plastic material. In addition, the Solex 30 PICT/2 carburettor was fitted to all 1500 engines, and the brakes, too, received attention as the rear shoes were increased in width from 30mm to 40mm.

The most striking change to the Cabriolet for the European market was the adoption of 12-volt electrics (implemented some time earlier for America-bound cars). Upgrading from 6 volts contributed to the eventual appearance of a number of accessories, such as 4-way hazard flashers, which were introduced from January 1968, and built-in reversing lamps (standardised from August 1969), as well as a heated rear window.

Following the annual summer shutdown at Wolfsburg, the Beetle chassis delivered to Karmann incorporated a cable-operated fuel filler flap and, to improve interior comfort, the front heating vents were made more controllable with the provision of lever-operated flaps, allowing a more directional flow of air. These cars were designated for the 1969 model year and could be identified by their extra cooling louvres – amounting to 28 in total and made up from four banks of seven vents – on the engine compartment lid.

Together with its different body structure and shape of hood, the Cabriolet's inherent problem of overheating was made all the more acute by installation of the 1500 engine; hence the need for the greater number of engine cover louvres and increased volume of airflow. The question of cooling was exacerbated even further when the hood was lowered. Moisture, too, was a problem which was never as serious on Saloon cars; to avoid the ingress of water to the hood's wooden base frame, and to prevent rot and damage

1979 saw production of a limited edition Cabriolet, the Triple White: white paint, white hood and white leather upholstery. These cars were also fuel-injected, in the interest of performance and lower emissions and, according to individual market specification, were fitted with catalytic converters. The Triple White Cabriolets were amongst the last Karmann Beetles to be built. This car, which was photographed in Georgia, USA, now resides in the UK. (Courtesy Martin McGarry)

in this area, the underside of the engine cover was equipped with a water drainage channel.

The American specification Cabriolet was to steal yet another lead over European market cars by adoption of the 1600 engine then installed in the Volkswagen Type 2 Transporter. In its 1600 guise, the Cabriolet boasted a 50bhp output with a displacement of 1584cc. A year later, for the 1971 model year, European Cabriolets also received the larger engine. Curiously, the model was designated 1302S.

Into the last decade

Although the Cabriolet still looked very much like the car that had originally appeared in 1949, it was, nevertheless, very different. Though the original doctrine was unchanged, reliability was the uppermost consideration, together with an overall design that appeared ageless.

Arrival of the 1600 engine ensured the Cabriolet's improved performance; the 1584cc displacement pushed top speed to well over 80mph (128km/h). This, of course, did not put the car in the sports car category, but neither did it belong there. Along with the new engine there arrived a series of specification changes that were completely at odds with the original design.

In place of the well-proven torsion bars for the front suspension, Volkswagen decided to adopt MacPherson struts, and it was this change that led the way to both the Cabriolet and the Beetle receiving a completely revised front-end layout. While Saloons experienced a relatively short production run of five years with MacPherson struts, Cabriolets retained the

Photographed in an American dock compound, waiting to be shipped to the United Kingdom, the 1979 limited edition Triple White Cabriolet is something of a rarity. (Courtesy Martin McGarry)

system until production ended in 1980. The rear suspension also changed and was supplied with double-jointed driveshafts as used on the Karmann Ghia and semi-automatic Saloons.

Along with the revised mechanical specification, 1971 cars also looked different; frontal styling was more bulbous and there was a huge increase in space for luggage under the front bonnet, made possible by using the space previously needed for the torsion bar suspension. It also allowed the fuel tank to be repositioned, whilst the spare wheel, instead of standing almost upright in the nose of the car, was laid flat on the luggage hold floor. The spare wheel, in its former position, had allowed the particularly attractive and novel tool kit, complete with its dish-shaped carrier, to be easily accessed. The wheel jack was also inconveniently moved, from its under-bonnet location to under the rear seat.

Although seemingly ideal at the time, the MacPherson strut suspension does have its drawbacks, especially for those owners whose cars have been subjected to excessive wear and tear and the ravages of corrosion to the coachwork. Whereas

torsion bars are highly durable yet relatively straightforward to replace, the integrity of MacPherson strut mountings is at the mercy of the condition of surrounding bodywork. In this regard, the floor of the front compartment is susceptible to rot and replacement of this panel is a major undertaking.

The 1302S, with its 1.6-litre power pack, was delivered with front wheel disc brakes as standard. Stronger bumper brackets were allowed for, and even a built-in towing hook on the left-hand rear bumper assembly was provided. If much of the criticism of Volkswagen Beetles had been answered by the revised layout at the front of the car, the real transformation was to the engine itself.

The principle of the Okrasa tuning kit, which had previously converted single-port engines to twin-ports for enthusiasts wanting their Volkswagens to go faster, was at last, as some enthusiasts would agree, used to good effect on the 1302S engine. A more efficient oil cooler was added to cope with the larger engine and higher sustainable speeds, but there was, however, a fundamental problem in respect of poor performance.

The Triple White Cabriolet, photographed before export to the United Kingdom.
(Courtesy Martin McGarry)

To the consternation of Wolfsburg's engineers and Volkswagen enthusiasts alike, the engine suffered flatspots, a matter made all the more worrying by the fact that the 1600 cylinder head was showing a tendency to crack. The problems with the 1600 engine were eventually overcome by drilling an additional hole in each of the two-cylinder heads: this was done in preference to designing a completely new engine. The 1600's crankcase used materials with better heat stability.

As an example of how technology and the modern world was catching up with the Beetle generally, a diagnostic unit was fitted to the engine bay for 1972 model year cars. Located at the top left-hand corner of the engine compartment, this electronic device, when plugged into appropriate VW equipment, enabled surveillance of all the major functions of the car's engine.

Modern also was the Cabriolet's interior styling, made all the more up-to-date by a 4-spoke steering wheel finished in soft-feel material as an aid to safety. If prospective customers thought the new steering wheel looked familiar, they were right;

it echoed that fitted to the Porsche 911, not to mention the somewhat bizarrely styled Volkswagen-Porsche 914.

From August 1971, cars exported to America were fitted with an exhaust gas recirculation system (EGR) to reduce harmful emissions, which specifically complied with legislation then in force in California.

By far the biggest change in late-model Karmann Cabriolets was the 1303S, announced in August 1972. Built for the 1973 season, the car sported a completely restyled windscreen which considerably improved forward visibility. Because of the windscreen's exaggerated curvature, the bonnet top had to be shortened, and this gave the car a significantly different appearance.

The restyling exercise for the 1303S wasn't confined to frontal appearance, as larger taillight clusters meant the rear wings had to be re-shaped to be more prominent. Neither did the interior escape attention; a new facia gave the car an ultra-modern look, especially with its oddly-shaped shroud ahead of the steering wheel, and single dial which incorporated

Of the later Cabriolets, the 1303 is sought-after owing to its specification and level of equipment. Depicted here is a concours condition, fuel-injection, USA specification Cabriolet, with energy-absorbing bumpers which were a requirement for American vehicles. (Courtesy Ken Cservenka)

speedometer, fuel gauge, odometer, etc. At each side of the facia, circular fresh air vents were a departure from the traditional dashboard.

The 1303LS – L for luxury and S denoting the 1600 engine – boasted features such as a cigarette lighter and clock, whilst, as optional extras, there was a whole feast of accessories. Sports steering wheels with three spokes drilled for lightness and appeal; a sporty steering wheel cover; rally seat covers and Recaro-Ideal sports seats could all be had by the owner who wanted to turn the Cabriolet into something even more special. A varied assortment of gauges could be obtained, including ammeters and rev-counters; a leatherette stone guard cover was produced, and so were fanfare air-horns, as well as a wide range of gearshift sticks in various patterns.

Alternators replaced dynamos on all 1600 Cabriolets and Beetles, but was a feature required on USA export cars, which enjoyed a fascinating little extra: shock absorbers built into the bumpers. The new impact-absorbing bumpers were designed to withstand the rigours of American parking and could accommodate knocks of up to 5mph (8km/h).

For a change, trans-Atlantic-bound cars were at design odds with their European counterparts; from August 1974, while American Cabriolets retained wing-mounted, front flashing indicators, the indicators on European models were transferred to a lower position and incorporated within the bumpers under elongated lenses.

The sought-after 1303; note the flawless white paintwork and matching hood. (Courtesy Ken Cservenka)

In order to meet US emissions legislation, all cars sold in America were specified with Bosch L-Jetronic fuel-injection systems as mandatory, and from 1976 through to 1979, catalytic converters were necessary for cars destined for California. The other states allowed Beetles and Cabriolets to operate on a non-catalyst system, since they could meet the Federal emission standards with use of L-Jetronic injection.

Finally, in 1974 for the 1975 season, the familiar worm and roller steering mechanism gave way to a rack and pinion system, which gave the cars a much more positive feel. The late Cabriolets were also the most prestigious and were treated to such luxury features as special interiors with comfort as the principle consideration, an example of which was front seat head restraints. One of the most revered limited edition Cabriolets was the Triple White, so-called because of its white paint, white hood and white upholstery, which was sold from 1977 through to 1979. An even more limited edition was the Champagne, which was also available from 1977. This was, in effect, a Triple White model with four thin gold stripes along the lower edge of the doors and quarterpanels, and a sand-coloured hood. In 1979, three different Champagne II models were made available, comprising the Triple White with gold stripes, another with a teal body with white hood and interior, and the third having a metallic rose body with white hood and interior. Not all was perfect in the traditional sense, though, as the familiar hood, with its horse-hair sandwich, was no longer a viable proposition and was replaced with one made from a foam-like material.

Modifications to the late Karmann Cabriolets were few and far between, especially once the Beetle had been superseded at Wolfsburg, in January 1978. The Cabriolet lived on after the Beetle for just under two years, and the last car left Karmann's production line at Osnabrück on 10th January 1980.

Der KdF Wagen

The Karmann Cabriolet and Karmann Ghia owe their beginnings to the KdF Wagen, which came to be known as the Volkswagen Beetle. (Author's collection)

One of the twelve Cabriolet prototypes from 1938. (Courtesy Volkswagen)

Little was it realised when this early English language brochure appeared, that the Beetle would become an international institution. (Courtesy National Motor Museum)

VOLKSWAGEN

Cabriolet

2 Sitzer

Cabriolet versions of the Beetle were originally built by two companies – Hebmüller and Karmann. The 1949 brochure in the top picture shows the two-seater Hebmüller. The brochure goes on to describe the early 2+2 Cabriolet in the bottom picture as a poem of shapeliness, elegance, fascination and vivacity. (Author's collection)

Ein Gedicht !

Formschön
Elegant
Faszinierend
Temperamentvoll

Mit Recht hat das Cabriolet viele Freunde

denn es bietet ihnen zu jeder Zeit das Schönste:
Freude an Sonne und Bergen,
angenehme Geborgenheit bei Wind und Wetter.

The Cabrio's interior was plush, although the side bolsters were shortlived. (Courtesy National Motor Museum)

This delightful publicity illustration for the KdF Wagen epitomised Hitler's dream of a national People's Car. (Courtesy National Motor Museum)

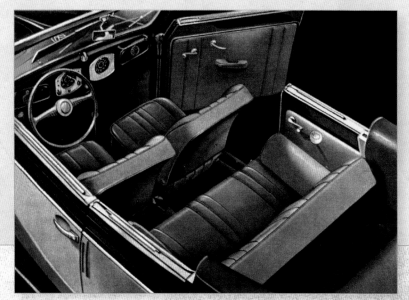

Modifications to the Cabrio's
mechanical specification generally
echoed those of the Beetle – and that
included the dash arrangement.
(Courtesy National Motor Museum)

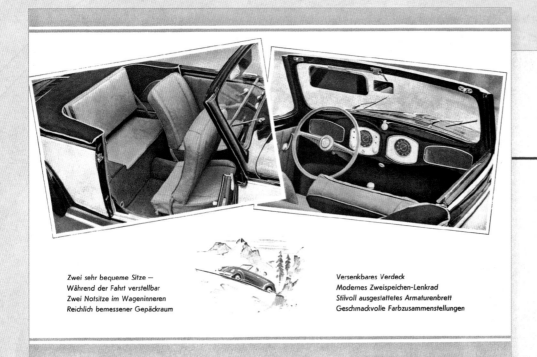

Zwei sehr bequeme Sitze —
Während der Fahrt verstellbar
Zwei Notsitze im Wageninneren
Reichlich bemessener Gepäckraum

Versenkbares Verdeck
Modernes Zweispeichen-Lenkrad
Stilvoll ausgestattetes Armaturenbrett
Geschmackvolle Farbzusammenstellungen

The charming illustrations above, from a 1949 brochure, show the style and comfort afforded by the 2+2-seater Cabriolet. (Author's collection)

Ernst Reuters was responsible for some wonderful Karmann brochure illustrations. This particular drawing dates from 1952. (Courtesy National Motor Museum)

IMPORT
PON's AUTOMOBIELHANDEL N.V.
ARNHEMSEWEG 2-14 AMERSFOORT TELEFOON 6545 (6 lijnen)

Das VW Cabriolet

Specially designed touring f
can be installed in place
of the normal bench type sea

Requirements - Readily Catered For

Many pleasing and usefull accessories can be provided at extra cost

Clock mounted next to
instrument unit

Whitewall tires
High-polish metal beadings

Press-stud-fastened cover to protect interior
of car from rain and sun

Armrest cushions
to match
upholstery

This Reuters illustration places emphasis on the Cabriolet's bespoke hood. The oval window and the split oval of the saloon were never features of the Cabrio. (Courtesy National Motor Museum)

Another evocative Reuters illustration showing the market for which the Karmann Cabriolet was clearly intended. 6000 cars per year were leaving Osnabrück for America by the end of 1955. (Courtesy National Motor Museum)

Reuters managed to give some of his brochure illustrations an almost surreal appearance, as with the Cabriolet shown here. (Courtesy National Motor Museum)

Beetle Cabrio flashing indicators were at first housed in small pods, as shown here. Later cars had larger indicator pods. Note this car's American specification bumpers. (Courtesy Martin McGarry)

Designated Type 15, the Cabriolet was seen as a carefree alternative to the Beetle saloon. This especially attractive Reuters illustration effectively demonstrates this. (Courtesy National Motor Museum)

The interior of the New Beetle. Even the much appreciated bud vase was included! (Courtesy Volkswagen)

Pictured at Fisherman's Wharf, this New Beetle Cabrio conversion is striking to say the least. A number of conversions emanated from America and Europe in advance of an announcement of an official VW Cabrio. Those enthusiasts who considered having their New Beetle converted needed to carry out careful research to establish that the end product would be properly engineered. Anyone contemplating the purchase of a conversion should be equally sure of the vehicle's history, which should include a comprehensive record of the conversion process. (Courtesy Tony Stokoe)

This interesting cutaway
clearly shows the body
structure of the New Beetle.
(Courtesy Volkswagen)

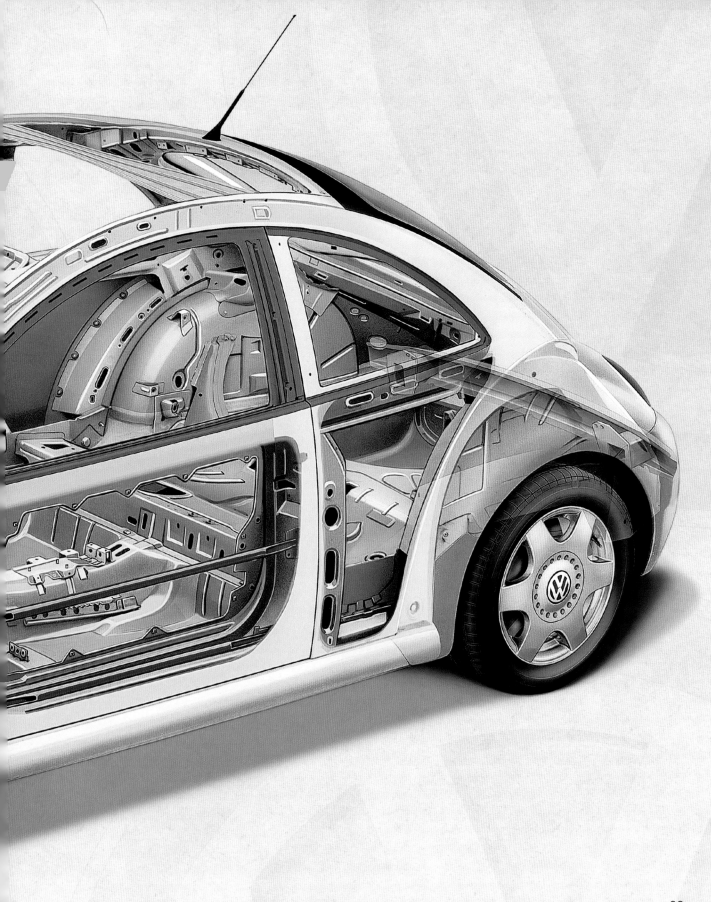

3 LIVING WITH A BEETLE CABRIOLET

Buying advice

What could be better than experiencing open-top motoring, feeling the breeze through one's hair and sensing the fragrance and sounds of the countryside? A romantic image perhaps, but it's one that more and more motorists are seeking when buying new cars, hence demand for the new Beetle Cabriolet remains buoyant.

It's not only buyers of new cars who are searching for the joys that Cabriolets offer. Motorists searching for classic cars are being drawn to convertibles, but it's not everyone who wants an out-and-out sports car. If one were to draw up a list of eligible cars offering saloon car comfort but with all the verve that a soft-top offers, the Beetle Cabriolet must surely be at the top.

Although it's now many years since the last air-cooled Beetle Cabriolets were built, there is, nevertheless, a high demand for examples of these cars in good all-round condition. What makes the Beetle Cabriolet so popular is its original build quality, pedigree, styling and renowned reliability. There's more of course, and when one includes the camaraderie that exists globally amongst enthusiasts, ownership of these attractive cars becomes all the more appealing.

Compared to some of the specialist cars of the era, the Cabriolet was produced in anything but small numbers. To place the Cabriolet's output of 331,847 vehicles in its proper perspective, the production figure of the Morris Minor Tourer totalled fewer than 75,000. However, in comparison to the 16 million Beetle Saloons built in Germany, Cabriolet production ensures exclusivity. In comparison with the total Volkswagen output, including Mexico and Brazil where the Beetle remained in production throughout the 1990s, Cabriolets account for around a mere 1.5 per cent of output.

Right-hand drive Cabriolets are relatively few and far between. Officially, the vehicle wasn't made available until 1955, so it's reasonable to assume that finding a left-hand drive car is a much easier task than finding a rhd specification model.

For the prospective owner, finding a good Karmann Cabriolet can be a minefield, especially if restoration is an issue,

Cabrios can often be found in reasonable condition in California, where this car – which was for sale – was pictured. (Courtesy Martin McGarry)

when there are serious questions to consider, such as whether the work will be done by the new keeper or a specialist. However well built in the first instance, the Karmann is prone to deterioration, the same as any car, and, due to the fact that it is a convertible, the ravages of time, weather and usage can have taken a substantial toll.

An important consideration with any Cabriolet, whatever the make, is the hood, and in this respect, the Karmann is no exception. Although superbly constructed originally, the Karmann's hood is nevertheless susceptible to all manner of vagaries, from weathering to vandalism – the latter being more of a problem than the former. If it's necessary to replace the hood, opting for a cheaper 'compatible' alternative is a false economy, as not only will it be contrary to the originally specified equipment, it also probably won't last as well or as long as an original item. A replacement hood is not inexpensive; it is a bespoke item,

Shipped to the UK from California, this is possibly the first snow ever to have settled on the car ... but it's almost certainly not the last! (Courtesy Martin McGarry)

meticulously crafted from the finest materials, and completely unlike anything found on popular convertibles, which in some instances have acquired a reputation for letting in water and hurricane-like draughts. In the closed position, the hood ensures that the Cabriolet is as snug as the Beetle Saloon, and leakproof as well.

Early Cabriolets will be all the more difficult to restore, if only because of scarcity of parts. This is not necessarily the problem it at first seems, as there are companies who specialise in the supply of Beetle and Cabriolet spares. It's just that some may be not as easy to locate as others, and may, as a result, command considerably higher prices. Another source of supply is a specialist that may be able to recondition the required component. Some parts are particularly obscure, such as the semaphore direction indicators, which are completely unique to the Cabriolet, and quite different to those found on the Saloon due to their having a slight curve to match the shape of the rear quarterpanels. A further obscurity is the rear view mirror: on the Cabriolet this was designed with a built-in hinge to allow for adjustment to see over the top of the hood when in the collapsed position.

Other differences to the Beetle Saloon of a significant nature are the front quarterpanels of early cars, which were furnished with cut-outs for the semaphore indicators, before the latter were transferred to the rear quarterpanels; and the engine compartment covers, which are special and had the cooling louvres punched into them due to the arrangement of the hood.

What ultimately makes the Cabriolet so different to the Saloon is its construction. The rear quarterpanels are double-skinned, which is why the rear windows can be wound down, and the body panel above the engine cover is strengthened to give sufficient support for the hood; so essential when in the open position. To compensate for the lack of torsional stiffness normally given by a steel roof, the Cabriolet receives its strength from supports built into the body. It is important to remember that it's the Cabriolet's body which is reinforced and not the platform.

When restoring a Cabriolet it's essential to know where all the strengthening areas are. Apart from the quarterpanels and rear section above the engine, there are reinforcement rails attached to the bottom of the sills and these are welded in place. Care should be taken to ensure other strengthening panels are in good condition: these are placed across the car, to form a platform (onto which the rear seat is mounted), and at the base of the B-posts.

Essentially, the running gear of the Cabriolet is similar to that of a Beetle. Although the VW flat-four is an extremely sturdy engine, there are specific points to watch for. The boxer engine is prone to oil leaks and these normally stem from the rocker covers and pushrod tubes. Check also for leaking oil where the engine joins with the gearbox, a leakage here could well mean a problem with the crankshaft main bearings; a further indication of this is too much play on the large pulley and excessive end float. The gearbox is very tough, but is hardly a proposition for a DIY rebuild and is best left to a specialist.

Thankfully, the Cabriolet has few vices of its own; the dreaded rot can set in as much as on a Saloon, but the extent may not be totally apparent on initial investigation. To buy a car and then find major restoration work is required is not only very

Properly restored, a Cabriolet is a very desirable classic car with few vices. (Courtesy Martin McGarry)

This photograph of a 1963 Cabriolet interior is indicative of how dashboard design changed over the years. Functional though it is, it lacks the charm of the early Cabriolet facias. (Courtesy Ken Cservenka)

expensive, but may easily destroy all the pleasure of ownership. It is important, therefore, to watch for tell-tale signs, but these are not always easy to spot. Weaknesses in the Cabriolet's strengthening can be investigated from underneath the car, at the limits of the reinforcing girders, where any signs of rust will be detected. If the rot is advanced – the most susceptible place is the box section at the rear – it's almost certain that the only solution will involve removing the body from the platform.

Late cars – those with MacPherson strut suspension – can suffer from rust on the underside of the front compartment. To replace a panel in this location is difficult enough, and it's sensible to also check the body structure around the suspension mountings as any work here will almost certainly be extensive and expensive. Torsion bar-suspended cars, usually, do not give the same problems as later models.

There are two other particular areas to investigate: the doors, especially where the upper section meets the side quarterpanels, and the panel between the hood and engine cover. The hood is anchored on a wooden section at its base and, in time, this is susceptible to rot due to the ingress of dampness from the hood itself. This can result in rust forming along the top of the valance, which, in the main, is confined to pre-1970 cars, manufactured before a drainage tray was fitted to the underside of the engine lid. Rust is the villain in the case of the doors and this can be seen forming along the upper edge, adjacent to the quarterpanel.

When looking at a Cabriolet there are a number of more general areas to investigate. Check the bumper mountings to ensure that the car has not been involved in a shunt; a vertical crack where the bumper meets the platform is a warning sign. Accident damage can also be detected by the way the engine and front compartment panels are installed; uneven gaps around the panels could indicate a poor repair. Rust may be detected around the front screen. If this is evident it could indicate blocked water channels and the rust may be more extensive under the surface.

Watch for rust around the door hinges, and also check the double-skinned quarterpanels, as it could be that condensation has resulted in rusting from the inside outwards. Look also at the floorpan for rust in the footwells and, while in this area, examine the floor under the battery housing. Jacking points should also be inspected, as should the front and rear axles; corrosion can occur at either end of the front torsion bars and in the area immediately above the rear suspension casing.

Heat exchangers, if in doubtful condition, can present problems with toxic fumes entering the car's interior through the heating pipes; make sure these are sound to prevent future problems.

When purchasing a Karmann Cabriolet, it's important to get as much evidence of the car's history as possible. It may be that previous owners kept a comprehensive log of all repairs and servicing, though it's just as likely that this documentation is missing. Not only is it best to check chassis and engine numbers with the original registration records, but also whether the car is known to the relevant owners' club.

The Cabriolet's rarity, compared to the Beetle Saloon, immediately puts the price of the car at a premium. Do not expect to pay a minimal price, even for a car that's in need of extensive refurbishment. Generally, Karmann Cabriolets command around twice the price of a comparable Saloon. Right-hand drive cars are notably more expensive than left-hand drive examples, purely due to availability, as are Hebmüllers and other specialist coachbuilt cars.

Specialist advice

Finding a Cabriolet is not difficult – choosing the right car may be more so. A good source of cars currently for sale are Volkswagen specialist publications, as well as the owners' clubs magazines and newsletters. The more general periodicals aimed at the classic car enthusiast will also, no doubt, have examples from which to choose. The internet, particularly eBay, is usually a good source for locating cars but care has to be taken in checking a vehicle's provenance. It is important to get as much information about the car, including seeing documents and accessing the car's history, as well as viewing detailed photographs, before committing to a purchase. Another course is to attend an auction, but, again, it's essential to view the car and glean as much knowledge of the vehicle as you can. Should you be in doubt as to a car's condition, it's worthwhile asking a specialist – or, at least, someone who has personal knowledge of these cars – to assess the vehicle on your behalf.

Having decided upon the most suitable car to purchase, it's more than likely the owner will, at some time, come into contact with one of the many Volkswagen specialists, whether it be as a source of parts, for routine servicing, or for a restoration project. Because of the impressive survival rate of Volkswagen Beetles generally, there is, happily, no critical shortage of mechanical components. To some extent this is due to manufacture (albeit in small numbers) of the Beetle Saloon in Mexico, in tandem for a time with the New Beetle. As far as the Cabriolet is concerned, it is the acquisition of body parts that presents the greatest difficulty.

If you don't have the practical skills to undertake restoration work, it is essential you entrust the project to a responsible and recommended specialist. Such specialists will almost certainly be known to other enthusiasts and the owners' clubs. Most specialists will be aware of cars for sale and some will have a selection of their own on offer. It is possible that particular specialists will be able to import cars from Germany or, more specifically, from the United States to Europe. The climate,

Even with lowered suspension, side skirts and minus engine cooling louvres, this roadster's styling retains an air of originality. (Courtesy David Sparrow)

This California-registered roadster is strikingly painted and has a white interior; detail trim items reflect the exterior colours of tangerine and orange over white. (Courtesy David Sparrow)

Customising the Cabrio

Rounded and cuddly, the Beetle Cabriolet is ideal for customisation. Some, however, consider customising to be totally unnecessary, choosing to preserve originality above all else. Whatever your opinion about vehicle originality, customisation of the Beetle and the Cabrio is part of a large worldwide industry.

The number of cars built, together with an impressive survival rate, has ensured that there is a keen market for customised cars, and it could be argued that, by doing so, old and unwanted or damaged machines are saved from being scrapped. Enthusiasts have a choice when considering customisation: some will want to undertake the project themselves, whilst others will be happier entrusting their vehicle to a specialist. The alternative is to purchase a car that has already been prepared. Whatever one decides, the choice of what to buy, and from whom, is endless. A glance through any of the specialist magazines will reveal a plethora of ideas, and classified advertisements can offer huge selections of cars.

When buying a car that has been customised, it is essential to ensure that all of the documentation relating to the work is available. Without such records, any purchase must be very carefully considered, and, in any case, advice should be sought from the relevant clubs and specialists before buying. Avoid a car that has not been converted to the highest of standards.

When entrusting a vehicle to a specialist it's wise to approach only those with experience and a good reputation. A lot of money can be at stake to have a car properly customised, and the enthusiast will rightly expect years of enjoyable motoring from it. Reputable specialists will be able to provide evidence of their work, and it's advisable to contact previous customers.

Possibly the most straightforward option, is to approach recognised specialists who will have a selection of customised cars for sale. Visit the specialists' premises and see for yourself the quality of work in progress and attention to detail. Have some pretty definite ideas about the type of customisation you want, and keep to a price. Several visits to any number of firms

especially in California, does mean it is possible to obtain a Cabriolet in the best possible bodily condition; as long as the bodywork is sound, the mechanical aspect of the car should not present too many problems.

To get the best comprehensive advice concerning all aspects of ownership, joining the appropriate enthusiasts' club is recommended; for details of enthusiasts' clubs and a list of specialists, check the appendices at the end of this book.

Right and below: Wizard Roadsters are popular among enthusiasts looking for vehicles that offer a degree of individuality with the purity of original design. (Courtesy David Sparrow)

may be necessary before choosing a vehicle, and take the time to talk to enthusiasts who already own customised cars

A particular point when choosing a car that has been customised is its provenance. The less experienced enthusiast might believe he is purchasing a Cabrio, when, in fact, the car is a saloon converted to a roadster. There is nothing wrong with this, as long as the customer is aware of what is being offered, and that the conversion and customising has been carried out to the best specification.

When considering DIY customisation, check that you have the necessary facilities, equipment, knowledge and expertise to do the job properly. Always be prepared for the project taking longer than expected, and costing more than originally estimated. Give considerable thought to what is required: will the engine and transmission remain as original? Is the suspension going to be lowered? Is there sufficient chassis strengthening – if not, what has to be done to ensure that safety and vehicle structure is not compromised? Are the parts necessary to undertake a successful custom conversion available,

The classic surroundings contrast with the arresting lines of this Belgian-registered roadster, left and below. The svelte shape of the car, as viewed from the rear, reveals a drivetrain that appears very non-original. (Courtesy David Sparrow)

The lowered suspension and absence of body furniture gives this Belgian roadster conversion a mean and moody attitude. Note the wide section tyres and the engine modification. (Courtesy David Sparrow)

Having American specification bumpers and partially enclosed rear wheelarches, this Belgian Cabrio still looks remarkably conventional compared to many customised cars. Some enthusiasts prefer just a hint of customisation to the more extravagant designs. (Courtesy David Sparrow)

and are they of the required quality? Are some or all of the original body panels to remain? What level of customising is planned for the cabin interior?

Finally – and, possibly, most importantly – is the cost. Keeping within a budget is not as easy as it might seem, especially when enthusiasm rules the wallet; always be prepared for unexpected costs and delays.

A visit to any of the many enthusiast meets around the world will reveal countless customised roadsters and cabrios. The choice of styles is endless, as this chapter's photographs show.

THE BEETLE REBORN

An icon of the twentieth century, the Beetle, adored by millions worldwide, is the car that refused to die. For years after its demise in Europe, the familiar egg-shaped car that gave a measure of independence to countless families who might not otherwise have afforded a motor vehicle, continued to be available in Mexico. For those enthusiasts for whom nothing but a Beetle would do, there remained the opportunity to acquire 'the real thing,' rather than a modern-day design, carrying the instantly recognizable VW emblem. Such was the enthusiasm for a car which the manufacturer considered had past its useful life, that VW began to believe it would be possible to resurrect the Beetle.

Ideas for a car that would emulate the success of the Beetle began in 1991, nearly two decades after the Golf had displaced it. To young Americans, the Beetle was symbolic of freedom and independence; a belief echoed around the world, including Europe and Australia. Deep within the Volkswagen organisation, a number of projects were being evaluated, including those with a retro theme, but which, nevertheless, employed cutting-edge technology. Slab-sided and angular designs were no longer popular with stylists, and the car-buying public eagerly responded to the subtle curves and smooth surfaces which had become the trend. It became apparent that it was possible to recreate a likeness of the Beetle, and incorporate its classic elements, without making it comical or cartoonish.

It was at Volkswagen's California Design Centre that the initial sketches were mapped. The relationship with the Beetle was instantly obvious, but what the stylists perceived was a concept so new that it would have been outstanding, even if the Beetle had never existed. The Volkswagen Group had established a design studio at Simi Valley, to the north of Los Angeles, in January 1991, in order to identify international trends at a formative stage, and to develop ideas for the American market in particular. By the autumn of 1991 the idea of producing a New Beetle was becoming a reality, and twelve months later authority was given for a couple of quarter-scale models to be made.

The personalities behind the New Beetle project were J Mays, head of the design studio, and Freeman Thomas, the Centre's Chief Designer. Both men had previous involvement with the German auto industry, Mays having formerly worked at BMW, and Thomas at Porsche. When he was recruited to work at Volkswagen, Mays was initially appointed to Audi, and Thomas, when he joined the company, was directed to VW. The two designers eventually met when they were posted to California to set up the Simi Valley Studio.

Outside of the Studio, the ideas that Mays and Thomas had discussed remained secret. There were very good reasons for this, as not everyone at Volkswagen shared their enthusiasm for a New Beetle and there remained a strong possibility that the project would be quashed. The directive from VW headquarters, for futuristic ideas and a retro theme – despite being linked to current and future technology – was going to have a difficult passage.

The fact that Volkswagen's market share in America plummeted during the early 1990s had everything to do with Mays and Thomas remaining steadfast in their belief that the New Beetle project could happen with the right backing. When they approached Hartmut Warkuss, Volkswagen AG Design Director, they found him not only supportive, but also keen to approve the submission of an outline plan which, he maintained, had to be conducted in absolute secrecy.

In the summer of 1992, Freeman Thomas was sent to Audi for a few weeks, to assist with a specific design project. Meanwhile at Simi Valley, work on the embryonic New Beetle remained dormant, although both Thomas and Mays discussed particular aspects of its design whenever possible. It was only after September 1992, when Thomas had returned to Simi Valley, that the project took a huge leap forward. With the building of quarter-scale models, the assignment became a serious study within the Volkswagen regime.

The New Beetle came about partly as a way of complying with California's strict criteria regarding anti-pollution and motor vehicle emissions. With manufacturers having to conform to

A huge response greeted the New Beetle concept car, Concept 1, at its unveiling at the Geneva Motor Show in March 1996. By that time, the project had been under development in California at Volkswagen's Simi Valley Design Studios for some five years: the brainchild of designers J Mays and Freeman Thomas. The New Beetle, launched in January 1998, encapsulated the essence of the classic Beetle, one of the world's best-loved motorcars, combining, as it did, nostalgia and modern technology. (Courtesy Volkswagen)

local legislation which demanded that two per cent of output be comprised of zero emission vehicles, development of the New Beetle was thus closely linked to environmental requirements. In Volkswagen records there is a proposal for an electric car designated the Lightning Bug. Instead of having a separate chassis, as did the original Beetle, the New Beetle was, from the outset, designed around the VW Polo floorpan. Only later was development continued using the Golf platform. The models created in the styling studio were wholly distinctive, and formed from the idea of amalgamating three 'cylinders': the front wings and wheels, the arched passenger compartment, and the rear wings and wheels. Initial proposals advocated separate front and rear wings in order to maintain more of an association with the shape of the original Beetle. Ultimately, that arrangement was disregarded in favour of partially integrating the wings with the frontal area to produce a completely modern image. It was not only the aesthetics with which the designers were concerned; they took build into account as well.

Styling and design, had, by necessity, to revolve around front-wheel drive, and so it was necessary to discreetly introduce a frontal air intake. Nevertheless, some fundamental acknowledgement to the Beetle's rear drivetrain was thought appropriate, and early ideas included the addition of cosmetic louvres sculpted into the rear hatch, beneath the window. Subsequently, the need for such detail was deemed unnecessary.

The New Beetle's styling characteristics had advantages in respect of customer use and satisfaction. Not only did the arched roof allow an amount of interior space unequalled by any other small or medium saloon car, but the bodywork,

and the wings in particular, could be easily repaired in the event of damage.

The two scale models that were made reflected each designer's individual styling preferences. Mays and Thomas had chosen to craft their own designs, and it comes as little surprise that the end products were decidedly similar. At first glance the models could easily have been thought identical, and only a detailed examination revealed subtle differences. The model built by Freeman Thomas was the more curvaceous; the side windows had rounded corners, and the panels were slightly more bulbous in shape. Mays' design had more acute lines and was characterised by windows with sharp angles. It was not only the external styling that the designers concerned themselves with. Close attention was paid to the interior, and that designed by Thomas was soft and rounded, with a definite retro theme. Mays' approach, however, was more geometric, with a rather stark appearance. Thomas' theme was the preferred one, although the Beetle character was evident: both designs featured a single pod directly in front of the steering wheel so as to suggest minimal instrumentation. Painted surfaces rather than vinyl cladding personified the original designs, and both designers found it necessary to add that charming but most essential ingredient, the bud vase.

Concept 1

In May 1993, detailed development of the New Beetle project had reached a point where Thomas and Mays were confident of progressing towards building a full-scale model. Hartmutt Warkuss was again consulted, and then treated to a high profile presentation in which the values of the original Beetle were recorded. Warkuss was then reminded of Volkswagen's once formidable American presence and, depressing as it was, how it compared to the then current situation. Ending on an upbeat note, the aspirations the New Beetle might achieve were thought provoking, to say the least. The strategy Thomas and Mays had conceived was compelling, and they deduced from Warkuss' enthusiasm that it was successful. In fact, the designers were able to impress Warkuss sufficiently for him to make an instant, but nevertheless rational, decision that activity be concentrated in making the project a reality.

If Hartmut Warkuss had ever agonised about convincing Dr Ferdinand Piëch, grandson of Dr Ferdinand Porsche, about the merits of introducing an all-New Beetle, he need have had no concern. Piëch, too, received the same brilliant presentation as had Warkuss, and within four months the project to develop the New Beetle – known within Volkswagen as Concept 1 – was official. All the more inspiring was the knowledge that the Volkswagen Board of Management had agreed to there being a full-scale Beetle design study ready in time for the January 1994 Detroit Motor Show.

When it was unveiled at Detroit, VW's Concept 1 was the undisputed star of the motor show. There remained, nevertheless, some opposition within the Volkswagen Group to resurrecting the Beetle ethos, the main concern being how a model with a retro theme would affect the company's reputation. This anxiety was not shared by America's Volkswagen dealers who, when they saw the model, voted unanimously for the car to go into production. Two months later, Concept 1 was the centre of attention at the Geneva show, where it was displayed in Cabrio form, this being the first time that such a design format had been publicly proposed. Any opposition to the New Beetle had by now evaporated, and everyone within Volkswagen accepted that production of the car was inevitable.

It was ironic that there was so much interest in Concept 1, as initial plans had called for it to be built around the Polo platform, Volkswagen's then smallest car. The Polo was neither certified nor sold in the United States, yet Concept 1 was the car that everyone clamoured for. There was, however, one serious problem. When Dr Piëch drove a prototype at the VW test track at Ehralessien, he was unimpressed. The car was too small, it did not handle as he had expected, and there was every reason to abandon the project. For the design team the years of work could have ended in disaster but, fortunately, Piëch refused to let his initial impressions affect his decision. He allowed development to continue using the Golf platform, the car that accounted for twenty per cent of Volkswagen sales worldwide, and which was a proven product in America.

There were several reasons for deciding to use the Golf platform. Work had already started on revamping the Golf

for a 1998 launch, and Concept 1 development fitted easily within that programme. The Golf platform would allow for a significantly larger car than that originally proposed: the wheelbase increasing from 92.1 inches to 98.9 inches and overall length by approximately a foot; the width grew from 65.1 inches to 67.9 inches. The weight increase was substantial, almost doubling from 1430lb to 2712lb, but the Golf's 2.0 litre engine would provide more than sufficient power. With the Golf certified for the US market, the New Beetle could be built at the Mexican assembly plant at Puebla, where Golfs and Jettas were constructed for North America. Building the car in Mexico meant economical delivery and lower labour rates.

Initial proposals were for the New Beetle to have a lesser mechanical specification than that of the Golf, such as drum brakes instead of discs. There was a danger that the New Beetle might become a novelty car and not a purposeful market leader, which Piëch did not want to happen. It was at Piëch's insistence that the car should share the Golf's running gear. With development transferred from California to Wolfsburg, Rudiger Folten was placed in charge of the project design team, and it was under his direction that the final form of the New Beetle emerged.

The fact that development was conducted around Golf technology instead of the Polo caused some disquiet among the motoring media. Fears were expressed about losing the ideology that was Concept 1, and, in answer to these concerns, Volkswagen lost no time in reassuring potential customers that the harmony between the old and New Beetle remained. Volkswagen went as far as to display a Golf-based, full-scale model of the revised Concept 1 at the 1995 Tokyo Motor Show. In Volkswagen terms, this was a re-dimensioned version of Concept 1.

Concept 1, which, by this time, was almost in its final form, was the subject of huge interest at the March 1996 Geneva Motor Show. With its usual razzmatazz, Volkswagen used the event to officially name the car the New Beetle, and at the same time launched a New Beetle website to satisfy the curiosity of Beetle fans around the world.

There were distinct detail styling differences between the original Concept 1 and that of the re-dimensioned version. Gone were the twin air intakes seen on the nose, replaced by a single large air intake beneath the protruding bumper; the false louvres below the rear window disappeared, and the radius-shaped corners on the windows were restyled. Rudiger Folten's view was that if the New Beetle was to be taken seriously, it had to have a fresh and meaningful appearance. The same philosophy extended to the car's interior. The facia was made more welcoming and less austere, although, fundamentally, the arrangement seen on Concept 1 remained, with instrumentation accommodated within a single pod. When he saw the finished interior, Freeman Thomas enthusiastically approved the modifications.

In the early development stages, it was anticipated that a Cabrio would be included in the New Beetle model range. Resources and development costs meant that, by early 2002, an authorised Cabrio version had yet to be announced. Concept 1 in convertible form was first shown at the Geneva Motor Show in March 1994. Initial design studies had been based on the VW Polo floorpan, but, eventually, it was decided to use the VW Golf platform. Following the January 1998 debut of the New Beetle, it took five years for Volkswagen to offer an official Cabriolet. If anything, the definitive car appears more Beetle-like than the prototype see here. (Courtesy Volkswagen)

Approval was given to revise the New Beetle's mechanical specification in August 1997, only a couple of months before the car went into production. Almost entirely Golf based, the New Beetle was tooled to employ all-round disc brakes, the one feature Dr Ferdinand Piëch had insisted the car should have. The change to disc brakes almost didn't happen, and even prototype cars used for evaluation and publicity were running with drum brakes.

When the New Beetle was officially launched in the United States at the Detroit Motor Show in January 1998, it was actually already in production, being manufactured alongside the original Beetle which, virtually handbuilt, remained available. A target figure of 500 cars per day had been agreed but, in light of huge

public and media response to the car, this figure was increased to 600 per day. In October 1998, the New Beetle made its European debut at the Paris Motor Show. Again, the car was received with massive applause, and production in Germany was scheduled to begin in December.

That the New Beetle would be voted North American Car of the Year at the January 1999 Detroit Show was almost a foregone conclusion. The car could not help but capture the imagination: its image immediately appealed to Beetle enthusiasts, as well as many of those motorists who previously might not have contemplated Beetle – or even Volkswagen – ownership. The shape was exciting, and the impression it made was one of delightful nostalgia and freedom from convention. The colour range available added to its appeal, the Cyber Green and Lemon Yellow in particular emphasising the cheeky curves just as nicely as the more predictable reds, blues, black and white. New Beetle publicity material unashamedly targeted the younger generation and the young-at-heart. Fun on the outside, serious underneath, was the marketing message, loud and clear. Skiing, snowboarding, surfing or cycling, the New Beetle accommodated all with the appropriate carrying accessories.

As soon as it was launched, customers around the world were eager to try the New Beetle. In the United Kingdom, left-hand drive models began to appear via private imports, and in April 1999 left-hand drive cars became officially available at Volkswagen dealerships. It was not until January 2000 that right-hand drive models were sold, the demand for the car increasing the UK allocation of New Beetles from 5000 to 8000 units per year. In August 2000, the 2.0-litre model was joined by an entry-level 102bhp, eight-valve, 1.6-litre version, with a slightly lower specification which didn't include air-conditioning, alloy wheels or R16 tyres (although these could be specified as options in lieu of standard equipment). Additions to the model range specification included four-speed automatic transmission, a 1.8T 150bhp high-performance saloon, and a manual-only 170bhp V5-engined super-Beetle variant. Turbo-diesel models were announced at the New Beetle's launch for availability in 2002.

Cabrio conversions

The fact that a Cabrio variant was not available when the New Beetle was introduced obviously came as a big disappointment to those customers who had previously owned a classic Beetle convertible, or who had set their sights on a New Beetle soft-top. Renewed interest in cabrios generally meant that a potentially wider market was not being satisfied. Having indicated from the outset that a convertible would be marketed, Volkswagen maintained that discussions within the VW Group regarding putting the variant into production were continuing. Ever since the New Beetle's launch, rumours and counter rumours regarding an official Cabrio were circulating, and, according to several sources, an authorised prototype was, in 2001, displayed in America, despite denial from Volkswagen. A number of dealerships in the USA referred to a March 2002 launch for the car, again something that Volkswagen denied. There were, however, a number of indications that Volkswagen had entrusted the eventual manufacture of an authorised Cabrio to Karmann.

Without an official VW Cabrio, it was only a matter of time before individual coachbuilders and conversion specialists, anticipating a demand from committed enthusiasts, set about offering their own saloon conversions. Several examples were seen in the USA and Europe, some employing better conversion methods than others. Some conversions initially appeared presentable, but close examination revealed a number of less than satisfactory aspects. Most problems were associated with underbody strengthening, something which – if not undertaken properly – could lead to future complications and disappointment. A number of European conversions were conducted by coachwork specialists in the former Eastern Bloc, where labour rates were substantially lower than those in Western Europe.

With the Beetle Cabrio always having had a popular following in the UK, a left-hand drive New Beetle Cabrio conversion was presented at the 2000 Birmingham International Motor Show. Following this, other examples were released onto the market – and not entirely with Volkswagen's blessing. In the USA, Volkswagen told its dealerships not to sell certain aftermarket conversions, and not to undertake warranty work on them.

At least one specialist, Kamei, the aftermarket accessories firm, tried negotiating with Volkswagen to produce a company-sponsored conversion. Despite VW recognising the car's potential, it foresaw a conflict of interest between Kamei and Karmann. Kamei's car was produced in time for the 1999 Frankfurt Motor Show, where the Beetster, as it was known, caused something of a sensation. That Kamei could have sold a substantial number of the conversions there is no doubt, but without official endorsement from Volkswagen, the project was not viable. Kamei did not build the Beetster, but commissioned the East German firm Beetle Revival to do the work. Beetle Revival had previously prepared a number of conversions on the New Beetle, including one example with a powered hood. In the Beetster's case, to acquire the essential speedster styling it was necessary to reduce the height of the A-pillar by one-third; then the floorpan was strengthened to compensate for the loss of the roof and a pair of roll-over bars were fitted. The tailgate was removed, and in its place a bootlid fitted, with hinges concealed under the new rear decking. Even though the suspension was stiffened and wider section tyres fitted, the ride quality of the Beetster remained completely acceptable.

In Germany, a firm called Beetlechose prepared a number of Cabrio conversions, and in the USA several examples were completed by Stramen (Richard & Lani Stramen) of Newport Beach California, and Newport Convertible Engineering (NCE), amongst others. As with all conversions, it's advisable to closely check the quality of work and to consult recognised experts for an opinion about a product's suitability.

In Britain, the leading conversion specialist Beetle-Bugs UK, located in Reading, Berkshire, was recognised for its conversions on a wide range of vehicles, to include the Range Rover as well as the classic air-cooled Beetle. Brian McCrorie, the director of Beetle-Bugs UK, sanctioned the concept of converting the New Beetle in the spring of 2000, and the first car to emerge from the firm was unveiled a year later on the 30th April 2001.

It didn't take long for Cabrio conversions to appear in the United Kingdom, courtesy of a variety of converters, some products being of better construction than others. British enthusiasts had to take care over the choice of converter, and in the case of choosing a completed conversion, establish that the finished product was properly engineered. The conversion pictured is that of Beetle Bugs UK, of Reading in Berkshire, a leading independent VW specialist at the time. (Courtesy Beetle Bugs UK)

When motoring journalists were invited to drive the car, they experienced a vehicle that was in every way satisfying: handling characteristics were correct, engineering exemplary and exterior and interior finish exceptional.

It took three to four weeks for Beetle-Bugs to prepare each Cabrio, which was tailor-made to customer specification. The body strengthening process didn't detract from the car being a full four-seater, nor was there compromise in luggage carrying capacity. The conversion process allowed for either a manual or powered hood to be fitted, as well as electrically operated rear side windows, rising from the quarterpanels in similar style to those fitted to the original Karmann Convertible. Such conversions were normally undertaken on new vehicles ex-works, but adaptations were offered on customers' own cars. It was Brian McCrorie's intention to have a stock of new car conversions ready for sale. The company, with its good reputation and healthy number of orders, supplied vehicles for export to countries such as Japan, Malaysia and Singapore, which required right-hand drive cars.

Beetle-Bugs conversions were carried out by highly skilled engineers, each benefitting from years of experience in the coachwork, engineering and automotive industries. They calculated every detail regarding the amount of strengthening required to ensure cars handled and performed as the manufacture originally intended. During the conversion process the interior of a vehicle was completely removed, to allow sufficient access to those areas requiring strengthening. Body painting was unnecessary after the conversion, and all areas that were worked-on were resealed to original condition and specification.

With the initial demand for the New Beetle, Volkswagen was reluctant to offer an official Cabrio version of the car, mainly because of the additional tooling costs. But, influenced by the number of Cabriolet conversions being offered, and the obvious demand for a factory Cabriolet, Volkswagen was

Continued on page 108

Right and below: When the New Beetle Cabriolet went on sale, some 80,000 orders were received. The retro look was liked by Beetle enthusiasts, and it was much appreciated by a wider clientele who had not previously considered Volkswagen or Beetle ownership. Not only was the car well built, it offered open-top motoring at a time when Cabriolets were becoming highly fashionable. (Courtesy Volkswagen)

It has been said within motoring circles that the New Beetle Cabriolet captures the essence of the original Beetle more so than the New Beetle Saloon. As a stand-alone car it has huge charisma and presence with its modern and curvaceous lines, a build quality that puts many other cars to shame, and all the ingredients for enjoyable year-round motoring. The car looks just as attractive with the hood lowered as it does raised, and the interior design is appealing, making the cabin a nice place to be. (Courtesy Ken Cservenka)

For the 2006 model year, Volkswagen gave the New Beetle Cabriolet (and Saloon) a minor face-lift. Immediately obvious is the restyled grille, modified sidelights and re-profiled headlights. The dash-mounted flower vase remained a feature. (Courtesy Volkswagen)

able to announce its new Beetle Cabriolet in the autumn of 2002 for the 2003 model year.

Of course, the announcement of the New Beetle Cabriolet was greeted with enthusiasm, for this was the car that Beetle devotees wanted. It wasn't only dyed-in-the-wool Beetle owners who clamoured for the car, but motorists wanting something different, chic and trendy, and who had not previously been loyal to the VW marque. Suddenly a whole new market potential was realised, particularly as retro-styling was the fashion, as were convertible editions of niche cars. That the car had, in reality, little to do with the original air-cooled Cabrio, other than a semblance of shape, seemed not to matter. This was the car in which to be seen driving, even if the platform and running gear

had been borrowed from the Golf hatchback, complete with the dated 115hp 2.0-litre petrol engine – albeit with a few minor modifications to give a smoother and broader range of power.

Volkswagen worked wonders with the Golf platform by giving it 35 per cent greater torsional stiffness than was the case with the air-cooled model. Safety legislation having evolved since air-cooled days, the New Beetle Cabrio was given a glass rear window and rollover protection courtesy of reinforced rear headrests that popped-up in the event of a tip-over. There were some cosmetic features – such as turn indicators incorporated within the side mirror housings, and a centre console housing the audio equipment – which were the precursor to modifications available for the Saloon.

Whilst the 2.0-litre engine was specified for US market cars, UK and European market vehicles were additionally available with the 1.6-litre engine. The model range widened with a 1.4-litre petrol version in the summer of 2003, along with a 1.9-litre turbodiesel, the sound of which some commentators likened to that of the traditional air-cooled unit, though from the front of the vehicle rather than the rear.

For the American market the New Beetle Cabriolet was extremely well equipped, the base GL version having air-conditioning, all-round anti-lock disc brakes, side-impact airbags, cruise control, power windows and mirrors, as well as power locks. A ten-speaker audio system was included, in addition to a tilt-and-telescopic steering wheel. Next step up, the GLS, sported optional automatic transmission, a power roof and fitted foglights, while the even plusher GLX had heated leather seats and rain-sensing wipers.

For Europe and the UK it was the 2.0-litre which got all the toys, including alloy wheels, air-conditioning, central locking, electric front windows, power steering, ABS, tinted glass, leather seats, and powered and heated mirrors.

Some 80,000 orders for the New Beetle Cabriolet were received by Volkswagen during its first year of production, on behalf of customers who considered it to be better looking than its saloon sibling.

Relatively few production modifications have been made to the New Cabrio, the most significant being announced in the summer of 2005 for the 2006 model year. Giving the car a facelift might be an overstatement, but it did have, in Volkswagen's terms, 'a discrete fine-tuning.' Volkswagen, conscious that the New Cabrio had achieved cult car status, was careful to retain the parallels to the historic Beetle, with its open top resting on the rear of the car, without it being a copy of the original Wolfsburg classic.

Externally, styling modifications were limited to a subtle redesign of the headlights, giving them a more oval shape. Sidelights, too, were reshaped so they were narrower and more angular, and taillights became more prominent with white-in-red circle indicators. All the more prominent, the integral bumpers – the front incorporating a radiator grille and fog lights, with the rear housing the new elongated fog and reversing lights – gave the car its sportier, more defined appearance. A new range of paint colours gave the Cabriolet a more vibrant and youthful look, and a range of wheel designs allowed customers the opportunity to give their cars a more distinctive and individual finish.

On the basic 1.4-litre petrol model, a manually operated weatherproof soft-top was specified, though electro-hydraulic operation was an option. On other models, automatic raising and lowering of the roof was a standard feature, taking just thirteen seconds to complete, the top folding to a Z-shape when in the open position. On all models, a cover protecting the open hood, and in the same colour as the car's interior appointment, was supplied; it was also possible to specify a folding and detachable rear screen to reduce air turbulence within the passenger compartment.

Revisions to the Cabriolet's interior amounted to several minor cosmetic changes, such as chrome bezels adorning instruments and vents which, together with a new range of upholstery designs, gave the car a more energetic character. One fitting that didn't change with the Cabriolet, was provision of the dashboard-mounted flower vase which has been a feature of the Beetle for such long a time.

The Cabriolet was shown to be one of safest open cars on the market when extensive rollover tests were conducted. Located behind the rear seatback, the rollover protection system is activated via a control unit when sensors determine the possibility of the car rolling over. Under such circumstances, two support columns pop-up and, together with the reinforced windscreen frame, protect all four seats. Front and combined head-side airbags are triggered at the same time to afford additional security.

A further aid to security and comfort, the Cabriolet is fitted with vibration-absorbing technology to ensure that steering wheel vibration and body movement (both of which are peculiar to convertibles of all types) are eliminated.

Five engine types were announced for the second series New Beetle Cabriolet, all of which were mated to five-speed manual gearboxes, except for the 1.6-litre which had the option of a four-speed auto 'box, and the 2.0-litre which could be specified with six-speed auto Tiptronic transmission. The base 1.4-litre engine, with its 0-62mph (100km/h) time of 14.6 seconds, provided a top speed of 100mph (160km/h) and an average fuel consumption of 40mpg (7.1l/100km); the 1.6-litre, a maximum of 110mph (178km/h) and 42mpg (7.7l/100km) fuel consumption using the five-speed stick shift. The 2.0-litre, when mated with the manual gearbox, gave 114mph (184km/h) and around 33mpg (8.8l/100km), but with automatic transmission the figures were reduced to 112.5mph (181km/h) and approximately 31mpg (9.2l/100km). The most powerful of the petrol engines was the 1.8 turbo, with its 0-62mph (0-100km/h) acceleration taking 9.3 seconds. Top speed was 125mph (202km/h) and a remarkable fuel consumption of 35mpg (8.1l/100km). The 1.9-litre turbodiesel propelled the car to 111mph (179km/h) and sipped fuel at the rate of 51mpg (5.5l/100km).

In 2010, seven years after the first series New Beetle Cabriolet went into production, and four years after the second series car was launched, it was time to bring production to a halt, in advance of a completely new design. Stories surrounding a new New Beetle had been circulating for some time, and various

This VW press photograph of the third generation Cabrio depicts a modern interpretation of the original car. More than anything, the message is the Cabrio's forever young and carefree image. (Courtesy VW)

unofficial images of a proposed model appeared at intervals, courtesy of the internet. Officially, a new Beetle was awaiting its debut in the autumn of 2010, but a cabriolet version was still some time away from being announced.

The second generation New Beetle made its official debut at the Shanghai Motor Show in April 2011, but it wasn't until October that year that the car went on sale in the USA. Customers in mainland Europe and the United Kingdom had to wait until April 2012 before the car was available. The new, New Beetle was designed by a team led by Walter de Silva, VW Group's Design Chief, and Klaus Bischoff, VW Brand Head of Design, who took styling cues from the original Beetle, as well as the Beetle Ragster concept, which was shown in Detroit in 2005. Longer, wider and having a marginally longer wheelbase than the outgoing model, second generation New Beetles were designed to have a more sporty, masculine and dynamic appearance.

It wasn't until October 2012 that Volkswagen announced the third generation Beetle Cabriolet, which was based on the recently introduced Saloon. With its sportier and more dynamic silhouette, together with a flatter roofline and more upright windscreen than previously seen, Volkswagen claimed the new, New Beetle Cabriolet's shape more resembled that of the original model. At launch, the car was available with seven engine options, from an entry-level 1.2-litre petrol to a lively 1.4-litre and a high-performance 2.0-litre, plus two diesels, a 1.6 TDI and a 2.0 TDI. The car made its debut at the Los Angeles Motor Show on 28th November, and went on sale in Europe and the United Kingdom in the spring of 2013.

However much the Beetle and its Cabriolet sibling are modernised, one thing that cannot be changed is the ethos of the original design which emerged more than eighty years ago.

I

PRODUCTION FIGURES TO 1980

YEAR	NUMBER PRODUCED
1948	3
1949	364
1950	2695
1951	3938
1952	4763
1953	4256
1954	4740
1955	6361
1956	6868
1957	8196
1958	9624
1959	10,995
1960	11,921
1961	12,005
1962	10,129
1963	10,599
1964	10,355
1965	10,754
1966	9712
1967	7583
1968	13,368
1969	15,802
1970	18,008
1971	24,317
1972	14,865
1973	17,685
1974	12,694
1975	5327
1976	11,081
1977	14,218
1978	18,511
1979	19,569
1980	544
TOTAL	**331,850**

II

SPECIFICATIONS

ORIGINAL MODEL SPECIFICATION

Karmann Cabriolet

Engine

Flat-four, ohv, air-cooled. Alloy crankcase and cylinder heads, cast iron barrels. Four main bearings. Bore/stroke 75mm/64mm, 1131cc. Compression ratio 5.8:1. Mechanical fuel pump, Solex 26 VFJ carburettor. Maximum power: 25bhp @ 3300rpm.

Transmission

Four-speed gearbox, no synchromesh. Gear ratios: 1st 3.60; 2nd 2.07; 3rd 1.25; 4th 0.80; reverse 6.60; final drive 4.43:1. Clutch: single dry-plate.

Brakes

Mechanical four-wheel system, cable operated; drums front and rear. Parking brake operating on rear drums. Hydraulic brakes from April 1950.

Suspension

Transverse torsion bars at front with twin trailing arms and double-acting shock absorbers. Transverse torsion bars at rear; trailing arms and swing axles; double-acting shock absorbers.

Steering

Worm-and-nut, 2.4 turns lock-to-lock.

Wheels and tyres

5.00x16 crossply.

Dimensions

Wheelbase	94.5in (2400mm)
Overall length	160in (4070mm)
Overall width	60.5in (1540mm)
Height	59in (1500mm)
Dry weight	1720lb (780kg)
Kerb weight	2558lb (1160kg)

Performance

Top speed	62mph (99.2km/h)
0-60mph (0-96km/h)	45 seconds
Max speed in each gear:	
1st	12mph (19.2km/h)
2nd	25mph (40km/h)
3rd	40mph (64km/h)

LATER MODEL ENGINE SPECIFICATION

Karmann Cabriolet

	1200	1300	1303S
Capacity (cc)	1192	1285	1584
Bore	77mm	77mm	85.5mm
Stroke	64mm	69mm	69mm
Comp ratio	6.6:1	7.3:1	7.5:1
Output	30bhp	40bhp	50bhp
Max speed	62.5mph	75mph	82.4mph
	100km/h	120km/h	131.84km/h

New Beetle Cabriolet

Production 2003-2010

Worldwide production 228,135
UK sales figures 19,633

Original specification (lhd)
Engine
Four-cylinder 2.0-litre petrol, 1984cc.

Transmission
Five-speed manual, fwd.

Performance
Top speed: 115mph/185km/h.
Fuel consumption: 32.5mpg/8.7l/100km (combined figure).

Dimensions
Overall length 4081mm
Overall width .. ..1724mm (with mirrors, 1836mm)
Height 1498mm

COLOUR	CODE	YEAR
Silver Beige	L277	61
Earth Brown	L571	63
Savannah Beige	L620	66-70
Black	L41	1949 on
Toucan Black	-	58
Atlas Blue	L338	58
Sea Blue	L360	60-71
Arctic Blue	L363	59-60
Pacific Blue	L398	60-71
Indigo Blue	L436	60
Polar Blue	L532	63-71
Ice Blue	-	61
Night Blue	-	61
Pearl Blue	-	56
Iris Blue	-	56
Diamond Grey	L243	58-69
Rock Grey	L264	60
Shetland Grey	L329	57-59
Pebble/Flint Grey	L440	60, 62-77
Slate Grey	L464	58-64
Alabaster	L473	58, 60-71
Sepia Silver	-	56
Bamboo	L241	58-59
Jade Green	L349	60
Sea Green	L381	61-63
Sargasso Green	L445	60
Beryl Green	L478	60-63
Emerald Green	L514	62
Hydrate Green	-	61
Nepal Green	-	61-63
Cadmium Red	L437	61-63
India Red	L451	54-55, 60
Paprika Red	L452	60-62
Pearl White	L87	58-67
Blue-White	L289	61-66
Cumulus White	L680	65-71
Manilla Yellow	L560	62, 65-71

Note: colour swatches are for illustrative purposes only.

APPENDIX IV

AT-A-GLANCE CHRONOLOGY

YEAR

1949	Production starts
1950	Adoption of hydraulic brakes
1951	Fresh-air vents fitted to front quarterpanels
1952	Synchro fitted 2nd, 3rd & 4th ratios
	Front quarterlight windows fitted
1953	More power provided by a 1192cc engine
1954	Rear lights enlarged on USA cars
	Other minor alterations
1956	Tubeless tyres adopted
1957	Larger rear window
1962	Improved brakes Type 3 345 launched
1963	New shape rear plate lamp
1965	1300cc engine fitted
1966	1500cc engine fitted
1967	New shape headlamps
1968	Double-jointed rear axles
1969	New indicators
1970	1600cc engine fitted
1971	Improved cooling
1972	New dash, windscreen and tail lights
1975-1979	No significant changes
1980	Production ends

SPECIALISTS & SUPPLIERS

Allshots Beetle Centre
Allshots Farm, Woodhouse Lane, Kelvedon, Essex CO5 9DF,
England
Tel: 01376 583295
Parts

Autocavan
103 Lower Weybourne Lane, Badshotlea, Farnham, Surrey,
England
Tel: 01252 333891
Fax: 01252 343363
Parts. Contact company for individual branch addresses

Beetle Exchange
Unit 40 Woolner Way, Bordon, Hants, England
Tel: 01420 487857
Fax: 01420 477907
Restoration and parts

Beetle With Care, Cares Garage
School Lane, Crowborough, Sussex TN6 1SE, England
Tel: 01892 653519/0850 573737
Restoration

Beetlelink
Unit D2 Preymead Farm, Badshot Lea, Farnham, Surrey GU9
9UT, England
Tel: 01252 326767
Parts, repairs, servicing and sales

Big Boys Toys
13 Breach Road, West Thurrock, Essex RM20 3NR, England
Tel: 01708 861827
Fax: 01708 863031
Parts

Bugmania
Unit 7 Cardiff Road Business Park, Cardiff Road, Barry, South
Wales
Tel: 01446 421954
Restoration, servicing and repairs

Continental Auto Spares
64 Haxby Road, York, England
Tel: 01904 610286
Tel: 01904 633060 (workshop)
Parts and repairs

Euro Car Parts
140 branches throughout the UK
Euro House, Fulton Road, Wembley, Middlesex HA9 0TF,
England
Tel: 0870 150 6506 (national mail order)
Parts

John Forbes Automotive
7 Meadow Lane, Edinburgh EH8 9NR Scotland
Tel: 0131 667 9767
Sales, service, repairs and parts

Just Aircooled
43 Hermitage Road, Bridlington, East York YO16 4HF
Tel: 0800 888 6287
Parts

Genuine VW Parts
29/30 Castle Street, Brighton, Sussex BN1 2HD, England
Tel: 01273 326189
Fax: 01273 321363
Parts

Henley Beetles Ltd
Unit 8, 167 Reading Road, Henley-on-Thames RG9 3DP,
England
Tel: 01491 579657
Restoration

Herinckx Coachworks
229-235 Fairfax Drive, Westcliffe on Sea, Essex SS90 9EP,
England
Tel: 01702 339979
Restoration and repairs

Karmann Classics
96-98 North Ease Drive, Hove, Sussex BN3 8LH, England
Tel: 01273 424330
Restoration, repairs and parts

Karmann Konnection
4-6 High Street, Hadleigh, Essex SS7 2PB, England
Tel: 01702 551766
Fax: 01702 559066

6 Grainger Road, Southend-on-Sea, Essex SS2 5BZ, England
Tel: 01702 601155
Repairs, service and parts

Kingfisher Kustoms
Unit 5 Oldbury Road, Smethwick, Warley, West Midlands
B66 1NU, England
Tel: 0121 558 9135
Fax: 0121 558 9791
Parts

Martin McGarry
Motorworks, Mansfield, Notts, England
Tel/Fax: 01623 656443
Imports and restoration, new and used KG parts

Megabug
Unit 3 Whiteheart Road, Plumstead, London SE18 1DG,
England
Tel: 020 8318 7333
Fax: 020 8855 4289
Parts

Midland Volks Centre
254 Ladypool Road, Sparkbrook, Birmingham B12 4JU,
England
Tel: 0121449 4748
Fax: 0121766 7577
Parts

Original Volkswagen Neuteile
Axel Stayber, Hannoversche, STR 41A, D-3455 Staufenberg,
Germany
Tel: 5543 94110
Fax: 5543 94112
Parts

Osterley California Classics
Tel: 0208 568 3837
Mbl: 0831 548930
Fax: 0208 568 6358
Imports (viewing by appointment only)

Stevens VW Dismantlers
Drakes Lane Industrial Estate, Drakes Lane, Boreham,
Chelmsford, Essex CM3 3BE, England
Tel: 01245 362020
Parts

Volksbits
56 Bristol Road, Gloucester GL1 5SD, England
Tel: 01452 414665

800 Pershore Road, Selly Park, Birmingham B29 7NS, England
Tel: 0121 472 4285
Mail Order Hotline: 087 05143 397

Volkscraft Classics
Drakes Holdings, Ferry Road, Fiskerton, Lincoln, England
Tel: 01522 595407
Repairs, parts and servicing

Volkshaven
Green Acre Farm, Hophills Lane, Dunscroft, Doncaster, South
Yorks DN7 4JX, England
Tel: 01302 351355
Parts

Volksmagic
111 Park lane, Oldbury, Warley, West Midlands, England
Tel: 012 541 2278 / 0860 632087/6
Parts and repairs

Volkspares
Branches throughout UK
National Mail Order Hotline: 020 8265 2030
Parts

VW Books
28 Longnor Road, Telford, TF1 3NY
Tel: 01952 245345
sales@vwbookscouk

VW Heritage Parts Centre Ltd
9-11 Consort Way, Victoria Business Park, Burgess Hill, West
Sussex RH15 9TJ, England
Tel: 01444 251270

VW Speedshop
www.vwspeedshop.com
Unit 12, Ackworth Road Industrial Estate, Hilsea, Portsmouth,
Hants PO3 6RY
Tel: 02392 679417
Parts

Wallhouse
Maypole Crescent, Darenth Industrial Estate Park, Erith, Kent
DA8 2JZ, England
Tel: 01322 347513

Westside Motors
391 High Road, Woodford Green, Essex IG8 0XE, England
Tel: 020 8505 5215
Mbl: 0831 580316
Restoration parts

Gary Wilkie
c/o Stroud Engineering & Welding, 200 Westward Road,
Stroud, Gloucester GL5 4ST, England
Tel: 01453 750960 / 822522
Restoration

Wizard Roadsters
497 Ipswich Road, Trading Estate, Slough, Berkshire SL1 4EP,
England
Tel: 01753 551555
Fax: 01753 550770
Conversion specialists

CLUBS

AUSTRALIA

There are numerous VW clubs throughout Australia but contact details are subject to frequent change. Check the latest details on the internet via VW Club Australia at www.clubvw.org.au

BELGIUM

Der Autobahn Scrapers
David Baland, 72 AV Prince D'Orange, 1420 Braine L'Alleud, Belgium

VW Keverclub Belgie VZW
De Volkswagen Keverclub Belgie VWZ, Lostraat 25, 9000 Gent.
Tel: (09) 238 38 91

For the many other clubs in Belgium visit www.vwkever.com

BRAZIL

Fusca Clube Do Brasil
Caixa Postal 60131, cep 05096-970 Sau Paulo/SP, Brazil
Tel: 55 11 2207071
Fax: 55 11 220 7771

Also visit www.fuscaclube.com.br

BRITAIN

Association of British VW Owners' Clubs
66 Pinewood Green, Iver Heath, Buckinghamshire SL0 OQH, England

Club VW
Contact Pat or Mac Howarth, Redditch
Tel: 01527 500933

Historic Volkswagen Club
Rob Sleigh, 28 Longnor Road, Brooklands, Telford, Shropshire TF1 3NY, England

Karmann Ghia Owners' Club
Astrid Kelly, 7 Keble Road, Maidenhead, Berkshire SL6 6BB, England

Type 2 Owners' Club
Phil Shaw, 57 Humphrey Avenue, Charford, Bromsgrove, Worcestershire B60 3JD, England
Tel: 01527 72194

Volkswagen Owners' Club (GB)
PO Box 7, Burntwood, Walsall, Staffordshire WS7 8SB, England

VW Cabrio Club
www.beetlecabrio.co.uk

VW Type 3 & 4 Club
Paul Howard, 9 Park Meadow, Doddinghurst, Brentwood, Essex CM15 OTT, England
Tel: 01277 822357

Wizard Owners' Club
Glynn Harper, 24 Laurel Avenue Kendray, Barnsley, Yorkshire ST0 3JA, England

FRANCE

Visit www.vwcabrioclubs.france

GERMANY

Andreas Sayn
Beethovenstrasse 49, D-51373 Leverkusen 1, Germany
Tel: 49 214 51295

IG VW Niederelbe
Iris and Eckhard Borstelmann, Weissenmoor 3, D-2167 Düdenbüttel, Germany
Tel: 49 4141 84233

Käferfreunde Leverkusen 1986
Norbet J Sülzner, Am Junkernkamp 7, D51375 Leverkusen 1, Germany
Tel: 49 214 52670

Käferfreunde Solingen EV
Petra Reichert, Borchertstrasse 12, D-42657 Solingen, Germany
Tel: 49 212 809953
Fax: 49 212 870162

Thorsten Bräuer
Meisenburger Weg 11, D-42659 Solingen, Germany
Tel: 49 212 46194

VW Käfer Cabrio-Club
F Otte, Weitkampweg 81, 4500 Osnabrück, Germany

Also visit www.vw-club.de

INDIA
BPPT VE Owners' Club
Drs Agus Pramudya, JL MH Tharmira No 8, Ged BPPT Lt 7,
Dikiat Jakarta, Pusat, India

Also search the internet for VW Beetle Club of Mumbai

ITALY
Maggiolino Club Italy
PO Box 11027, Saint Vincente, Italy
Tel: 39 48 0931

NETHERLANDS
Keverclub Nederland
Gerard Wilkie, Postbus 7538 5601jm, Eindhoven,
Netherlands

Luchtgekoelde VW Club Nederland
Van Geerstraat 7, 2351 PL Leiderdorp, Netherlands

Volkswagen Cabriolet Club Nederland
vwcabrio.nl

NEW ZEALAND
VW Owners' Club
PO Box 12-538, Penrose, Auckland 1642, NZ
www.vwownersclub.co.nz

PORTUGAL
VW Clube De Viana Do Castelo
Contact Apartado 524, P 4901 Viano do Castelo, Codex
Portugal

SPAIN
Club Clasicos Volkswagen De Alicante
PO Box 420, E 03080 Alicante, Spain
Tel: 34 65 20 0777

SWEDEN
Air-coolers Vasteras
PO Box 3070, S-720 03 Vasteras, Sweden

Bugrunners
Lena Lilliehorn, Box 1141 Jarnvagsgatan 8, S-581 11
Linkoping, Sweden

USA
56-59 Karmann Ghia Registry
Jeffrey P Lipnichan, 961 Village Road, Lancaster, PA 17602,
USA
Tel: 717 464 0969

Limbo-Late Model Bus Organization International
PO Box 2422, Duxbury , MA 02331-2422, USA

Society of Transporter Owners
PO Box 3555, Walnut Creek, CA 94598, USA
Club Hotline: 510-937-SOTO

Split Bus Club
Gerry Morgan, 2452 O'Hatch Drive, San Pablo, CA 94806-
1466, USA

Vintage Volkswagen Club of America
817 5th Street, Cresson, PA 16630, USA
www.vwca.com

Volkswagen Club of America
www.vwclub.org

For further information, see listings in Volkswagen magazines
or contact the Association of British VW Owners' clubs –
see page 120

BIBLIOGRAPHY

Advertising the Beetle
Compiled by Daniel Young, Yesteryear Books

Beetle: Chronicles of the People's Car volumes 1-3
Etzold, G T Foulis

Essential Volkswagen Karmann Ghia
Laurence Meredith, Bay View Books

Illustrated Volkswagen Buyers' Guide
Peter Vack, Motorbooks

Karmann Ghia 1955-82
Brooklands Books

Karmann Ghia Coupé & Convertible
Malcolm Bobbitt, Veloce Publishing Ltd

Original VW Beetle
Laurence Meredith, Bay View Books

Small Wonder
Walter Henry Nelson, Hutchinson

The VW Beetle including Karmann Ghia
Jonathan Wood, Motor Racing Publications

VW Beetle Convertible 1949-80
Walter Zeichner, Schiffer Publishing Co.

VW Custom Beetle Colour Family Album
Sparrow, Veloce Publishing Ltd

VW Treasures by Karmann
Jan P Norbye, Motorbooks

Volkswagen Beetle
Marco Batazzi, Giorgio Nada Editore

Volkswagen Beetle
Bill Boddy, Osprey

Volkswagen Beetle Coachbuilts and Cabriolets 1940-60
Keith Seume and Bob Shail, Bay View Books

Volkswagen Beetle Colour Family Album
Sparrow, Veloce Publishing Ltd

Volkswagen Beetle: The Car of the 20th Century
Richard Copping, Veloce Publishing Ltd

MAGAZINES

Air Cooled Classics
aircooledclassicsmagazine.com

Autocar
www.autocar.co.uk

Motor
motoring.ninemsn.com.au

Practical Classics
www.practicalclassics.co.uk

Ultra VW
www.ultravw.com

Volksworld
www.volksworld.com

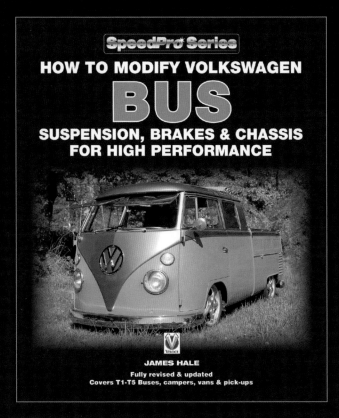

INDEX